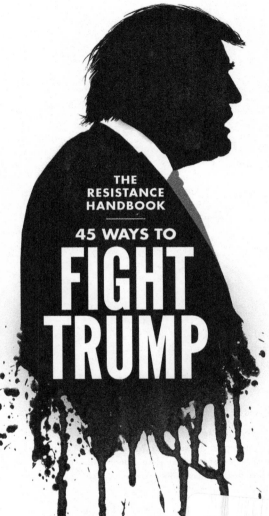

THE
RESISTANCE
HANDBOOK
———
45 WAYS TO
FIGHT
TRUMP

MARKOS MOULITSAS & MIC

DISRUPTION
BOOKS

AUSTIN   NEW YORK

Published by Disruption Books
Austin, TX, and New York, NY
www.disruptionbooks.com

Distributed by Disruption Books

For ordering information or special discounts for bulk purchases, please
contact Disruption Books at info@disruptionbooks.com.
Editor: Matthew Lewis
Cover design: Chris Bilheimer | Bilheimer Design
Text design: Sheila Parr

Print ISBN: 978-1-63331-017-9
eBook ISBN: 978-1-63331-018-6
First Edition

CONTENTS

INTRODUCTION

THERE IS A DIVIDE in the Democratic Party, but it's not between supporters of Hillary Clinton and those of Bernie Sanders. It's also not "the establishment" versus "outsiders." Those who persist with that dichotomy aren't just fostering unnecessary enmity between natural allies but are clinging to a simplistic plot line that has more in common with fake news than actual reality.

So what is this existing divide among Democrats? It's between those who *oppose* Trump and those who *resist* him and his regime. That may seem like trivial semantics, but it's actually a distinction with a huge difference.

In politics, the "opposition" assumes that the ruling powers are legitimate, and that their group or faction represents a "democratic minority" of public opinion. The loyal opposition acts as a check against the "tyranny of the majority," as John Adams once wrote, counterbalancing the powers of the ruling regime. The opposition intentionally differentiates itself from the majority, with the hope of building support for its values and objectives among the populace; but it can also find strategic opportunities to work and compromise with the majority in pursuit of the national good.

In normal times, that's what the losing party does—oppose the legitimate, democratically elected winner.

These are not normal times. Donald Trump is not the legitimate president of the United States, thus opposition is insufficient. Relentless resistance—using any lawful actions to stymie, harass, delay, and obstruct—is the only option.

DEMOCRACY FOR ME, BUT NOT FOR THEE

At this point, the electoral math has been well studied and combed over: Trump received nearly three million fewer votes than the popular winner of the election, Hillary Clinton. The Electoral College—an antiquated system designed to protect the property rights of slave owners—elevated the loser to office. It is the second time this century that this immoral, irrational, and undemocratic system has crowned an unworthy ignoramus and undermined our democratic values as a nation. And we clearly didn't learn anything from the debacle that was George W. Bush, since here we are again.

Of course, the deep flaws in our democracy aren't limited to the White House. In the Senate, the 48 Democrats in the "minority" have received, collectively, *23 million more votes* than the 52 Republicans in the supposed "majority." Why do the Dakotas, with their combined population of 1.6 million, have four senators, while California, population 38.8 million, has two? Why does Wyoming, with a population of 584,000, have two senators while Washington, DC, population 659,000, has zero?

The situation is no better in the House of Representatives, which is so heavily gerrymandered by Republicans that Democrats would have to win the House national popular vote by over *eight points* just to have an even-odds chance of retaking the chamber!

Our republican (lowercase "r") form of government is entirely predicated on the notion of proportional representation, but our current system is neither proportional nor representative.

During the 2016 campaign, Trump repeatedly complained that the system was rigged—and he was right! By any standards of democratic fairness, our system for electing presidents and members of Congress is objectively rigged to maintain Republican control of government. As our national demographics shift to increasingly multicultural urban values—and away from rural white conservative values—this rigging threatens to further undermine the legitimacy of our democracy.

BLOCK THE VOTE

Those antiquated, built-in institutional advantages Republicans enjoy prove we aren't living in a legitimate democracy. But even with those undemocratic structural flaws, Republicans *still* can't win elections in a fair vote—and so they engage in systematic voter suppression efforts, designed to reduce voting by people of color, women, and young voters.

It's no accident that Trump's victory hinged on narrow margins in Wisconsin, Michigan, North Carolina, and Pennsylvania. After GOP takeovers in the 2010 Republican wave, all four states systematically weakened organized labor—a key component of the Democratic electoral machine. They also made it harder for urban voters—a key component of the Democratic electoral coalition—to cast their votes through such mechanisms as strict voter ID laws and the reduction of polling stations in communities of color and college towns. As giddy Wisconsin Republican state senator Mary Lazich crowed after the passage of that state's voter ID law, "Hey, we've got to think about what this would mean for the neighborhoods around Milwaukee and the college campuses."

And yet, those institutional and electoral advantages were *still* not enough. In the months leading up to the 2017 election, an entire ecosystem of fake news sites sprang up to distribute a special brand of crazy. Meanwhile, Republican officials reportedly met with the *Russian intelligence agencies* later accused of causing damage to Democratic campaigns. As we write this, more than a handful of high-level Trump administration officials and Republican operatives are under investigation for colluding with Russia during the election. Meanwhile, as if all this weren't absurd enough, the FBI director leaked information on the bogus Hillary Clinton email investigation, while keeping mum about the FBI's investigations into the Trump campaign's Russian ties.

When the dust settled, after running the most hateful, xenophobic, racist, sexist, and anti-Semitic campaign in American history, and despite losing by any reasonable, democratic measure, we're to accept that Donald Trump "won"?

Sorry, but no.

We cannot accept the results of an illegitimate election won by an illegitimate candidate by illegitimate means. And as such, Democrats and progressives cannot consider ourselves the "opposition," opposite the petty tyrants and pennyweight dictators who rule today's GOP. Remember, opposition lends legitimacy to their illegitimate gains. An opposition crafts counterarguments in the hopes of gaining a seat at the negotiating table and rallies its supporters behind the idea that "next time we'll get more votes."

We *already* got more votes—and would have won even more had it not been for the Republican cheating. That makes *us* the majority. And yet, here we are, ruled by a *tyranny of the minority* that cheated us out of our deserved democratic victory.

We are not the opposition. We are the *resistance.*

NO QUARTER TO GIVE AND NO TIME TO LOSE

It is time for all-out, uncompromising resistance against the tyrannical instincts of Trump and the GOP, and support for our nation's disenfranchised majority. We must refuse any efforts to normalize Trump, his regime, or his party. We must be unyielding in calling out the injustice of our system, we must organize to fix its structural flaws, and we must fight tooth and nail to limit the risk of permanent damage to the essence of our democracy.

Whether Trump survives his entire term or not, these next four years will be the most important in the modern history of liberalism. They will feel painfully long. We will face a relentless assault on everything we hold dear: civil rights, women's rights, LGBTQ rights, environmental protections, criminal justice and police reform, immigrant rights, housing and transportation policy, health care policy, worker rights, electronic freedom and privacy—the entire progressive agenda is in the cross hairs. Trump's ascension to the White House gives the GOP the opportunity to attack and undermine the very values that shape who we are and how we view our country. And we will suffer defeats. A lot of them.

But if we've learned anything during Trump's first one hundred days, it's that his incompetence is our opportunity. We can fight and win, despite the GOP's majorities. So our first and most urgent task will therefore be to continue fighting to limit the damage. We need to hold our ground on policy, from protecting Obamacare and Planned Parenthood, to minimizing the horrors of forced deportations and racist travel bans, to stemming the inevitable carnage to the environment, working people, and families.

Perhaps more important, in addition to critical policy fights, we must limit the damage *to our culture*. It is *not* okay that an overt bigot gets rewarded with the presidency. It is *not* acceptable that someone who brags about "grab[bing women] by the pussy" gets elevated. People as racist, sexist, and anti-Semitic as Trump and his gang of brownshirted cronies have *no legitimate role* in our nation's public life: the United States is a nation of equal rights and protections *for all*, not just the privileged few who happen to be "acceptable" to Klan sympathizers like Attorney General Jefferson Beauregard Sessions.

The Trumpist movement's shameful bigotry must be confronted and banished from our culture, and urgently so: as long as such hateful beliefs are considered an acceptable part of our national discourse, we will fail to achieve the American ideals of equal protection and freedom for all. You cannot extend basic health care *to all* while disenfranchising and systematically oppressing the African-American community. You cannot provide free college to America's youth while deporting kids for being brown. And you cannot claim to care about families when the word "family" itself follows a narrow definition imposed upon 325 million Americans by a radicalized religious minority.

Having to fight to reestablish these self-evident truths is painful but necessary. It is also a task that will take much longer than a single election cycle, and one at which we are inexcusably behind in making progress.

OWNING OUR WEAKNESS

This part of Trump's victory is 100 percent on us: we, as a movement, never built the intellectual, activist, and electoral infrastructure we needed to support our candidates and issues; Republicans have been building theirs since the 1960s. It's the reason why a hateful ignoramus such as Trump could win without a real campaign, while Democrats need a transformative political figure like Barack Obama to win—despite having an electorate that agrees with us on most issues!

Wealthy white oligarchs like the Koch brothers, the Mercers, Sheldon Adelson, and Pete Peterson have spent billions of dollars building a network of organizations designed to promote their own personal financial interests; the Tea Party organized grassroots conservatives around elections; and a never-ending river of money has expanded the massive universe of conservative media outlets. They already had Fox News, Rush Limbaugh (and the entire AM radio dial), and dozens of magazines, astroturf think tanks, and websites. Did they really need to dump tens of millions more into *Breitbart*? Maybe not, but they did so anyway, and it paid huge dividends.

Meanwhile, liberals bought into the fiction that CNN and the *New York Times* were "liberal," even as those very publications led the charge in promoting fake news about the Clintons' non-scandals. At one time, the *Times* had two dozen reporters on the email story, with more digging into the Clinton Foundation—and how many reporters at these so-called liberal outlets were diving into Trump's shady dealings? The *Washington Post* had *one*—David Fahrenthold—who just won a Pulitzer for his legitimately outstanding reporting. There should've been dozens of Fahrentholds.

But these types of publications could never serve as a counterweight to the Right's partisan political media machine. *It's not their job.* The Left's own media outlets, such as *Daily Kos*, never stood a chance—on volume alone, we're getting crushed. As any marketer or advertising executive could tell you, it's not the best product that wins, it's the product with the best go-to-market strategy. Our movement has fallen back on the assumption that our ideas are good enough to win on the merits. But we're hardly even trying to promote our ideas, and when we do so, we always try to "compromise" with conservatives—people who don't share our values, who will never vote for our candidates, and who mostly act to water down or destroy every policy idea we bring into the political forum.

So while it's legitimate to bemoan the media for its irrational and messianic centrism and the impact of this bogus "centrism" on our ideals, we have to be honest about our own shortcomings as a movement: we have done a poor job rallying and organizing our core base. Obama inexplicably let his massive Organizing for America email list—thirteen million strong—atrophy. The Clinton campaign was breathtakingly inept, believing its own flawed data models over the increasingly panicked voices from campaign staff and volunteers on the ground. We have *tens of millions* of unregistered potential voters all around the country, particularly in communities of color, because the party's predominantly white donors don't prioritize or even understand the value of empowering these communities.

Our weaknesses don't end with our shallow grasp of field organizing. We don't come close to matching the Right's leadership development capabilities, youth mentoring, candidate recruitment, or candidate training. Our wealthy donors don't fund partisan endeavors; if anything, progressive donors cede the battle before it's begun by recoiling at the very idea of partisanship! And, adding insult to injury, the circular firing squad that formed around the Sanders-Clinton battle exposed the wide chasm between the party's communities of color and its white, mostly male "socialist progressive" faction.

Four years isn't enough time to fully build out the infrastructure we need to support a steady drumbeat of progressive ideas, but it's enough to kick-start those efforts and inspire a new generation of volunteers and donors to flood into the movement. This is our chance to pick ourselves up from the maws of last year's punishing defeat and build something new—and enduring—that can transform progressive politics for generations.

NO INFRASTRUCTURE

Imagine the alternative universe where Hillary Clinton won the election. She'd be president; we'd continue to improve upon Obama's tenure; that open Supreme Court seat would have an actual liberal on it, flipping control of the high court—and all that would be amazing! But every first-term president loses significant congressional seats in the first midterm of their presidency, and the inevitable infighting among the Left ("Hillary is a neoliberal corporate shill!") would further exacerbate that trend. Democrats would get walloped in congressional elections in 2018, falling even deeper into both the Senate and House minorities.

Perhaps more ominously, given the structural weaknesses of the progressive movement, we'd continue losing ground in state legislatures. If Republicans gain control of *one more state legislature*, they can call a Constitutional Convention and rewrite the Constitution to their liking—enshrining Trumpist Republicanism, with its doctrinaire bigotry, misogyny, and voter suppression, into the most sacred document of our democracy.

We'd lose governor and legislative races in states key to redistricting after the 2020 census, potentially entrenching Republican majorities in the House through *2030*. Those state-level Republican majorities would continue to do what they've been doing, but on steroids: making frontal assaults on workers' rights, women's rights, LGBTQ rights, minority rights, and access to the voting booth. For whatever good Clinton would've managed to accomplish at the top, we would've been routed down the ballot.

A Clinton victory, while infinitely preferable to our current predicament, would have obscured these deeper political vulnerabilities. Trump's win has not only unmasked the Republican Party for what it is—an aging white racist rump of a party still fighting the Civil War— it has also shown us how much more we, as progressives, need to do to advance our vision.

FROM DESPERATION TO INSPIRATION

Trump is inspiring millions of us to enter an existential fight for our political future. If we fight with focus, purpose, and commitment, we can come out of this much stronger than before. In a weird way, Trump may be the best thing to happen to liberalism since the New Deal.

To capitalize on the opportunity embedded in Trump's threat, we have to do everything we can to minimize the damage to public policy and our culture, while simultaneously building the infrastructure our movement so sorely lacks.

The Resistance Handbook offers a guide to get us through the next four years—and beyond. After Trump's victory, pretty much everyone with experience in political activism was swamped by their less political friends, who came to us and asked, "We did X, Y, and Z . . . *now* what do we do?" We hope this book provides some useful and actionable guidance on this question.

We believe we can emerge from this four-year nightmare more powerful, effective, and resilient than we've ever been. We believe we can channel the energy building against Trumpism, and use it to build an enduring political coalition that wins elections and transforms our nation well into the future.

We know there's a lot of hard work ahead, but it is our duty and honor to take on this task.

We are the new American Resistance.

SECTION I

RESIST TRUMP AT ALL COSTS

1

BRAND TRUMP AS A WEAK LOSER

RECOMMENDED RESOURCES
Don't Think of an Elephant! by George Lakoff
The Political Brain by Drew Westen
@Trump_Regrets

DONALD TRUMP rode a wave of populist discontent—and a badly outdated electoral system—to the White House. Along the way, he made a raft of absurd promises:

- He promised to build a border wall—with *Mexico* paying for it.
- He promised to tear up trade agreements and use his supposed negotiating prowess to give Americans better deals.

- He promised a health care "plan" that would cover *everybody*, and do so cheaper, and do so without damaging "freedom".
- He promised to say the words "Islamic terrorism" over and over again, which, he promised, would melt away the forces of ISIS and single-handedly destroy terrorism.

He would accomplish all that and more because he was the strongest ever. His quack doctor proclaimed Trump the healthiest ever. He certainly considered himself the smartest: "I comprehend very well, okay, better than I think almost anybody." And all those babes by his side? Why, he was the most virile! According to him, he was the embodiment of strength and success. America would win so much that we would get tired of all that winning!

We liberals made comedic sport out of attacking Trump—he made it so easy, and we are all so clever. We called Trump a narcissistic, moronic megalomaniac with zero grasp of reality. We branded him as a cruel, friendless sociopath, with a legendary trail of bankruptcies, failed businesses, and duped investors. We dutifully noted his moral decrepitude, racism, misogyny, and homophobia. And we ridiculed his egotism and hubris, as he repeatedly declared that he, and he alone, could fix America's problems.

We threw all that at the wall . . . and it stuck! His popularity was perpetually in the gutter. Trump went into the final weeks of the election with the worst approval ratings of any candidate in the modern era.

And yet . . . all those things we considered liabilities, his supporters perversely saw as *strengths*. He wasn't afraid to say what they were all thinking (the bigotry, the nativism, the disdain for knowledge and science), and hey, how could someone so rich be anything *but* strong?

Meanwhile, Trump didn't have to come up with a litany of complex and varied messages to brand and undermine his opponent. He did it with a single word: "crooked." The "crooked Hillary" meme was concise, direct, and focused; it reinforced all of Clinton's liabilities—real and perceived. It gave voters—both Trump supporters, fence-sitters, and the most rancid Bernie Bros—a simple heuristic to use to think about their voting choices.

It was textbook propaganda, executed to perfection, and it worked: Trump defined his opponent in the minds of both voters and the media, and in so doing, owned the election narrative.

The Resistance has to be better than Trump at this game. We can't keep throwing everything at the wall and hoping it sticks; a thousand slurs and insults aren't enough to do the man proper justice—and they also don't work! So let's focus on the character traits that he finds most offensive and that directly undermine his supporters' impression of their president: call him the "weak loser" that he is.

FOCUS ON THE CHARACTER TRAITS THAT HE FINDS MOST OFFENSIVE: CALL HIM THE WEAK LOSER THAT HE IS.

A WEAK LOSER WHO LOSES, AND IS WEAK

Trump pretends he won the election by historic margins, yet he lost the popular vote by nearly three million votes; his Electoral College margin was the weakest since George W. Bush's in 2004. Democrats Barack Obama and Bill Clinton both received larger Electoral College wins—and had *substantially* larger inauguration crowds to Trump's never-ending (and pathetically public) distress.

Not long after taking office, Trump, in his first foray as commander in chief of the armed forces, ordered a Navy SEAL commando to his death in a botched raid in Yemen—which he allowed to proceed even *after* its secrecy was compromised. But he couldn't take responsibility for his blunder. He blamed Obama. He blamed the military. He blamed everyone but himself. Strong men like him never fail!

The pattern has repeated itself through the course of Trump's presidency, and it's clear: when confronted with the reality of his losses, Trump can't handle it. His narcissism and pride are merely covers for his low self-esteem. Inside the facade of that pasty orange rind, he knows the truth: He *really is* weak. And he *really is* a loser.

Trump is only rich because his daddy gave him millions to launch his career—but he was still too much of a loser to even match the returns of the stock market. He drove multiple companies to bankruptcy, including, somehow, *a casino*. What kind of a loser do you have to be to lose money running a casino? During one Ohio campaign stop, the Secret Service sprung into action as a protester stormed the stage. Trump's weak, panicked reaction stood in stark contrast to Clinton's calm, cool demeanor during a similar situation.

Faced with the real challenges of running the United States, Trump is completely out of his depth—and his weakness is coming to the fore.

- He's backed off on his boastful demands that Mexico pay for his border wall. *Weak.*
- He failed to repeal Obamacare. *Weak.*
- His two attempts at Muslim bans have failed to pass judicial muster. *Loser.*
- He yielded to China after accidentally/intentionally straying from the official "one China" policy regarding Taiwan. *Weak loser.*
- He yielded to China again, backing off his campaign promise to label that country a currency manipulator. *Weak.*

- Mounting evidence revealed in several prominent publications links his campaign to Russian intelligence, making him a puppet of the Kremlin (not to mention Russian intelligence meddling via Wikileaks). *Weak.*
- When Russian president Vladimir Putin wasn't pulling the strings, Trump's Svengali adviser President Steve Bannon was (and Trump hates it when we call Bannon president). *Really weak.*

Trump doesn't have any family living with him in the White House, so he roams its empty hallways at night in his robe. *Loser.* He really, really cares what people say about him on cable news. *Weak.*

In fact, despite having congressional majorities, Trump ended the first one hundred days of his presidency without a single major policy or legislative victory to his name. He promised to be the strongest of strongmen, but this weak loser ended up in his place. Sad.

As the Resistance, we need to make sure that every time Trump's name comes up, we remind people that his name isn't "President Donald Trump." It's "Weak Loser Donald Trump." (Experiment with variations! "Loser Donald Trump" sounds great, too.)

It won't just feel good to call the weak loser president a weak loser; it will help ensure that Donald Trump is never again elected president of the United States.

2

IMPEACH TRUMP!

RECOMMENDED RESOURCES

CitizensForEthics.org
ImpeachDonaldTrumpNow.org
Corrupt.AF

WEAK LOSER Donald Trump is not a legitimate president. In addition to the well-reported facts about vote counts and Russian meddling, from day one, Trump has repeatedly confirmed that his love isn't for America and *all* its people—only for those who supported him and continue to support him, regardless of his incompetence and recklessness. He isn't president of the United States of America; he is only president of Whoever Kisses Donald Trump's Ass.

But being a weak loser with low self-esteem is not illegal—and while it helps to be clear that Trump is a weak loser, to get him out of office, we have to make the case that he broke the law. Thankfully, we have sufficient evidence to call for his impeachment, so let's call for his impeachment! Along the way, we can do a lot to undermine his presidency, weaken his cabinet, and shred his fragile political coalition.

DEATH BY A THOUSAND CUTS

Recent history offers us valuable lessons in the power of calling for the impeachment of a sitting president. Despite having *zero* evidence of illegal acts, Republicans relentlessly pursued President Bill Clinton's impeachment. The fishing expedition that led to the Lewinski scandal began with a failed $100,000 land deal in Arkansas (pocket-lint-type money for Trump), traipsed through false accusations of murder in the White House travel office, and zigged and zagged through another half dozen wild conspiracy theories before finally landing on Monica Lewinsky.

The key here: Republicans were willing to stoop as low as necessary to damage Clinton politically, undermine his credibility, and thus slash his chances of enacting meaningful, long-term legislation. Each time the Republicans failed to prove Clinton did anything wrong, they made up a new excuse and continued their pursuit. And it worked! The DC political media, always hungry for a scandal, breathlessly and credulously reported on every new made-up Republican outrage—and all the American people heard on their TVs was "scandal-ridden Clinton White House."

And what were the consequences of this bogus meme? Well, for starters, Hillary Clinton's effort to enact single-payer health care failed; the GOP retook the House in 1994 in a wave election built, in part, on the armature of phony scandals; and, of course, George W. Bush, a class clown who couldn't tell the difference between Iraq and Saudi Arabia, ascended to the White House, in large part due to the "scandal fatigue" invented by Republicans and dutifully echoed by lazy reporters. (In many ways, Hillary Clinton's inability to get a fair shake from the Very Serious People in Washington stemmed from the bogus character attacks against her and her husband throughout the 1990s.)

The Resistance gets to follow the same playbook, but with one significant difference: Trump is actually guilty of real constitutional violations. So, it's our job to equate the Trump presidency with law-breaking. If we're effective, we might even get *Republicans* to flee his vicinity. And that will take persistent highlighting of his high crimes against America.

> **IT'S OUR JOB TO EQUATE THE TRUMP PRESIDENCY WITH LAW-BREAKING. IF WE'RE EFFECTIVE, WE MIGHT EVEN GET REPUBLICANS TO FLEE HIS VICINITY.**

THE HUNT FOR RED NOVEMBER

The case for Trump's impeachment isn't just an academic exercise; understanding the depth of Trump's post-inauguration corruption and ensuring everyone around you is equally educated are critical to stopping him in his tracks.

So let's start with Russia, and its extensive meddling on behalf of the Republicans in the 2016 elections. It's clear why they did so—they viewed Trump as a weak puppet stooge, easily manipulated (unlike Hillary Clinton). As confirmed by the FBI, Russian intelligence broke into both Republican and Democratic computer networks, yet selectively leaked only Democratic material through their Wikileaks allies. (The Republican material may yet be used to blackmail the White House and complicit Republicans in Congress.)

Virtually all of Trump's inner circle has been tied to Russia. A partial review of those connections includes:

- **Paul Manafort,** Trump's first campaign manager, signed a $10 million deal with a close ally of Putin in order to secretly advance Russian president Vladimir Putin's interests in the Ukraine; he also received $12.7 million in secret payments from Ukrainian politician Viktor Yanukovych, a close Putin ally.
- **Michael Flynn,** Trump's short-tenured national security adviser, resigned after revelations of his possibly traitorous relationships with Moscow. (As reported by Media Matters, *New York Magazine,* and more, Flynn has also demonstrated close ties to white nationalists and Nazis in the United States).
- **Carter Page,** an oil industry consultant who worked for years in the Moscow office of Merrill Lynch, was one of Trump's top foreign policy advisers. He resigned his post after he got caught lying about meeting with Russian businessmen during a 2016 Moscow visit. BuzzFeed later reported that Page met with a Russian intelligence agent in 2013.
- **Jared Kushner,** Trump's son-in-law, has extensive ties to Russian oligarchs, including potentially billions of dollars in loans for his shady real estate deals.
- And, of course, consummate Texas oilman **Rex Tillerson,** Trump's secretary of state, was awarded Russia's Order of Friendship medal in 2013, presented by Putin himself. Under Tillerson's leadership, Exxon established substantial business dealings with Russia—and may have violated sanctions against Russia imposed by President Obama for its invasion of Ukraine; the oil giant urgently needs access to Russian capital and oil and gas markets.
- The list goes on . . .

We have an unprecedented situation in which the administration of the president of the United States was staffed, funded, and promoted, in part, by a foreign power. And Republicans, who made Russia hatred the bedrock of their foreign policy for generations, can't even pretend to care! So it's our job to remind Republicans, every day, that they are puppets—every one of them—of the Russian regime.

As Dan Rather wrote about the extensive Russian ties, "We may look back and see, in the end, that it is at least as big as Watergate. It may become the measure by which all future scandals are judged. It has all the necessary ingredients, and that is chilling."

The potential that Trump is a foreign agent working on Russia's behalf is, by itself, grounds for impeachment. But Trump being Trump, there's always more.

THE UNITED STATES OF TRUMP INC.

The Emoluments Clause (article 1, section 9, clause 8) was written into the Constitution to bring an end to the kind of rampant corruption that plagued governments during the time of our nation's founding. The relevant part of the clause states:

> *No Person holding any Office of Profit or Trust under them, shall, without the Consent of the Congress, accept of any present, Emolument, Office, or Title, of any kind whatever, from any King, Prince, or foreign State.*

An emolument is defined as "a salary, fee, or profit from employment or office." So is Trump profiting from his office? The case is open-and-shut.

Foreign powers are hosting their events at DC's Trump International

Hotel, or at Mar-a-Lago in Florida, to better ingratiate themselves with him. After ten years of fighting a trademark application for his name in China, the government finally granted it to him—immediately *after* he reiterated support for a one-China policy (sorry, Taiwan!). To make clear just how transparent the Chinese wanted to be with their "gift" to Trump, Chinese law actually *explicitly bans* trademarks that are "the same as or similar to the name of leaders of national, regional, or international political organizations."

There are his frequent golfing trips to his resorts, where his entourage, Secret Service protection, and foreign visitors must pay for their rooms (and even golf-cart rentals!)—profits benefiting the Trump Organization, naturally. Same with the security staff at Trump Tower in New York protecting Trump's family, because they refuse to move to DC and live in the White House. And with Trump refusing to disentangle himself from his business dealings in any real way, it's clear he's profiting directly from his office.

Finally, Trump has a habit of hurling baseless accusations, such as this Tweet accusing Barack Obama of illegally wiretapping him: "How low has President Obama gone to tap my phones during the very sacred election process. This is Nixon/Watergate. Bad (or sick) guy!" Defamatory speech—or speech intended to harm an individual, without evidence of wrongdoing—is not protected by the First Amendment. That sort of defamation is amplified when it's the government hurling false accusations, amplified even more when coming from Trump himself. Thus every deranged accusation Trump levels against his enemies, without proof to back them up, is another impeachment count.

The case for impeachment is ironclad, based on a clear reading of the Constitution. Yet, there won't be any impeachment hearings until 2019, at the earliest, because Republicans in Congress have zero interest in upholding the law of the land. The same crowd that spent millions of taxpayer dollars investigating Hillary Clinton for *legally* having her own email server have now conveniently found more important things to do than investigate Trump's unconstitutional self-dealings or Russian ties.

Meanwhile, on the very day that we turned in the final edits of this book to our publisher, Donald Trump fired James Comey as the director of the Federal Bureau of Investigations. This brazen attempt to stifle the bureau's multiple investigations into Russia involvement in the 2016 elections and among Trump's inner circle (and maybe Trump himself) was so brazen, it made Richard Nixon look like a smooth operator. *He literally fired the guy investigating his administration for treason.* So let's go ahead and throw in an "obstruction of justice" charge to the articles of impeachment.

Without any outside mechanisms to hold Trump accountable, the only weapons we have at our disposal are the congressional elections of 2018. Until then, call for Trump's impeachment every chance you get, educate people around you about his gross violations of the law, demand Democratic congressional candidates adopt impeachment as part of their platform—and then organize and activate to win those elections.

The American people are fairly reliable at rejecting political leaders they see as corrupt; the job of the Resistance is to ensure that the corruption in the White House and Republican Congress is front and center in the minds of voters when they enter the voting booth.

Then, come 2019, we can finally have a House of Representatives willing to hold our president accountable for his crimes against our nation.

3

CALL CONGRESS—THEN CALL CONGRESS AGAIN

RECOMMENDED RESOURCES

CallMyCongress.com
CallYourRep.co
IndivisibleGuide.com
OneCall.today
ResistanceinYourPocket.com
Resistbot.io
TheSixtyFive.org
WhatDoIDoAboutTrump.com

REPUBLICANS BEGAN agitating for the repeal of the Affordable Care Act the second it passed into law. And over the following seven years they never stopped or wavered in their commitment, using the law as a cudgel to sabotage Obama's presidency. They branded it as "Obamacare," then claimed it created "death panels"; warned of the rationing and out-of-control costs that, of course, never came; claimed it would destroy jobs and the economy, which it never did; and blustered about all the "freedom" that would be lost, whatever the heck that meant.

In total, the GOP voted *fifty-four times* to repeal the law, and Trump seized on that conservative fixation over the law, promising during his presidential campaign to replace it with something better: "We're going to have great plans. They're going to be much less expensive and they're going to be much better because the Obama plan is unaffordable and it's a disaster."

So it was safe to assume that, having won the White House while holding on to the House and Senate, Republicans would quickly and easily kill Obamacare once and for all. And they didn't dally. After laboring (for several hours) on his and Trump's "repeal and replace" bill, Republican House speaker Paul Ryan dutifully rammed it through the committee process and brought it to the full House for a vote. The Republicans' forty-four-seat majority should've made passage a fait accompli.

But then a funny thing occurred. Ryan ran into a buzz saw of citizen opposition so fierce that the improbable happened: It took Republicans three serious attempts before Republicans were able to pass their House bill. What emerged was a monstrosity so hateful—even turning things like asthma, cesarean births, and sexual assaults into "pre-existing conditions" without guaranteed coverage—that Senate Republicans immediately declared the House bill dead on arrival and set out to to design their own. The public backlash against House Republicans was so fierce, the liberal groups *Daily Kos*, Swing Left and ActBlue collectively raised over $4 million against yes-voting endangered Republicans within 48 hours of the vote. People fighting cancer, sexual assault survivors, and other Americans took to Twitter to decry a law that would strip them of health insurance. The town halls of yes-voting Republicans were angry, charged events. Devoid of any real momentum, Senate Republicans quickly indicated that they were in no hurry to pass a bill of their own.

And through it all, all Democrats, even the most conservative, remained a steadfast "no." This hasn't always been the case. A groundbreaking study by Christopher Skovron of the University of Michigan and David Broockman of the University of California Berkeley found that Democrats objectively believe their constituents are more conservative than they actually are. Why? Because conservatives have historically been more aggressive in calling, writing, and showing up at town halls.

How could this be? The answer is simple: good, old-fashioned organizing. During the GOP's first health care repeal attempt, people mobilized in unprecedented fashion, flooding Congress with phone calls that ran fifty to one opposing the Republican plan. New York Democratic representative Daniel Donovan said calls to his office were a thousand to one in opposition to Trumpcare. But opposition was near-universal across the country, even in Republican districts. Kentucky Republican representative Thomas Massie tweeted, "275 oppose vs 4 support #ObamaCareLite. Phone calls to my office from constituents over last two weeks. Why are we voting on this?"

Massie's district voted for Trump by a thirty-six-point margin. And he stuck to his "no" vote to the bitter end, on a bill that passed by just four votes.

NINETY PERCENT OF SUCCESS IS SHOWING UP

Despite controlling all three branches of government, House Republicans—with their big 44-seat majority—spent weeks trying before passing Trumpcare, and these calls were a huge reason why. How and why did calls and protests work to stymie and slow the GOP's repeal efforts?

- **They reinforced squishy Democrats.** Democrats objectively believe their constituents are more conservative than they actually are because those people are the most aggressive in calling, writing, and showing up at town halls. We've done a poor job of building up Democratic backbones. Massive phone efforts on our behalf are political calcium. They build spines.
- **They influenced swing-district representatives.** Elected officials in highly competitive districts are particularly sensitive to public opinion. A small number of highly motivated people could legitimately doom their reelection chances.
- **They created strange bedfellows.** Representative Massie didn't actually care what his constituents thought. If an outright repeal vote came to the floor, he'd vote for it in a heartbeat, dooming thousands of his own voters to a lack of health care, and in some cases, death. But by citing the phone call tally, he could pretend that his position came from a noble deference to the will of his district. It was bullshit, but so what? It worked.

Ezra Levin, Leah Greenberg, Sarah Dohl, and several other former congressional staffers saw these tactics used to great effect by Tea Party groups. So after Trump's popular vote loss/victory, they put together the Indivisible Guide, from which we will be borrowing heavily in the pages ahead. Its authors, more than most, understand the power of tactics such as making phone calls. "[Coordinated calls] are a light lift, but can have an impact," they wrote. "Organize your local group to barrage your [members of Congress] with calls at an opportune moment about and on a specific issue."

Any time is a good time to call your legislator (whether a member of Congress, state legislator, or city council person), but the effectiveness of such calls rises dramatically when part of a broader, coordinated campaign. You'll know when it's time to call—activist groups you belong to will email you with info (so join some groups!), or you'll see it on your Facebook or Twitter feeds, or you'll simply pay attention to the news and know what topics your elected officials are focusing on. At that point, it's time to act. These steps have been taken from the Indivisible Guide:

1. **Find your legislator's phone number.** Activist organizations may provide this to you via email or Facebook, or give you tools to automatically connect you to the right person. You can use CallMyCongress.com to find your congressperson. Some googling around should help you find state and city elected officials.

2. **Have a single point to make.** "The question should be about a live issue—e.g., a vote that is coming up, a chance to take a stand, or some other time-sensitive opportunity," states the Guide. "The next day or week, pick another issue, and call again on that."

3. **Ask to speak to the person who handles the issue you want to discuss.** So if you're calling about health care, ask to speak to the health care staffer. Now, the person answering the phone likely won't do this and will just take down your comment. So call back on a different day and ask, "Hi, can you confirm the name of the staffer who covers [immigration/health care/etc.]?" Staff will generally tell you the name. Say "Thanks!" and hang

up. Ask for the staffer by name when you call back next time. (Those Indivisible folks are wily!)

4. **If directed to voicemail (most likely result), leave a message**, then follow up with an email. They probably won't call you back, so keep sending emails until you get a response. And if you get no response, you can then tell the world that they are dodging you.

5. **Take notes of your conversations.** Write down direct quotes as much as possible. Feel free to tell the world what you hear, and compare notes with other activists, to see if there are any discrepancies in what they're telling constituents. If you have a media contacts list, keep them apprised of what you're being told. Tweet it out. Post on Facebook. Blog it at places like *Daily Kos*, Medium, and the *Huffington Post*.

NO "SAFE SPACES" FOR BAD POLICY

What if your legislator is in a safe district, either too liberal or too conservative to care about what you think? Your calls *still matter*. "The reality is that no Member of Congress (MoC) ever considers themselves to be safe from all threats," states the Guide. "No one stays a MoC without being borderline compulsive about protecting their image. Even the safest MoC will be deeply alarmed by signs of organized opposition, because these actions create the impression that they're not connected to their district and not listening to their constituents."

"EVEN THE 'SAFEST' [MEMBER OF CONGRESS] WILL BE DEEPLY ALARMED BY SIGNS OF ORGANIZED OPPOSITION, BECAUSE THESE ACTIONS CREATE THE IMPRESSION THAT THEY'RE NOT CONNECTED TO THEIR DISTRICT AND NOT LISTENING TO THEIR CONSTITUENTS."

Calls to hostile members are also important. As noted above, it could give an ideological foe a handy excuse to join your cause, even if for the wrong reasons. And if nothing else, flooding the offices of hostile legislators ties up staff, making them unable to work on whatever bit of damaging legislation they're focused on. As one Senate Republican staffer noted to the conservative *Washington Examiner*, "I definitely got behind on my legislative responsibilities because every time I'd look away from my healthcare messages, there would be 100 or 200 more." Remember, resistance means harassing and slowing the enemy down so that he (and with Republicans, it's mostly hes) can do the least amount of damage.

So make those phone calls. From the earliest days of the Trump regime, we've already seen how effective they are.

4

GO TO TOWN HALL EVENTS

RECOMMENDED RESOURCES

CouchActivism.org
IndivisibleGuide.com
RecessToolKit.com
ResistanceManual.org
TownHallProject.com

THE KOCH BROTHERS and Fox News enthusiastically encouraged the Tea Party to harass members of Congress into opposing President Obama's progressive agenda. At town halls, at their offices, even at their homes, Tea Party "patriots" would physically intimidate their representatives and senators into doing their bidding. Arizona Democratic representative Gabby Giffords was shot in the head, and another six people were killed, including a nine-year-old, and thirteen more injured by an antigovernment shooter at one of her constituent events.

Tea Party gatherings were always raucous affairs, generating a flood of media coverage—particularly local coverage, which is usually the most important market for elected officials. The coverage, along with the physical presence of loud, angry, sure-to-vote constituents, knocked legislators off their game. It also fueled additional Tea Party protests, as other hard-core conservatives came out of the woodwork, inspired by what they saw in the news.

Video snippets of elected officials fleeing Tea Partiers were solid gold, giving conservative activists evidence their tactics were having an impact. The phenomenon snowballed, building on itself through the painful passage of the Affordable Care Act—and planting the seeds for the Republican Party's massive election victories in 2010.

How big was that victory? Republicans gained six seats in the Senate to take the majority. More impressively they won 63 House seats to recapture the chamber, the largest gain since 1948. They haven't relinquished the House since. They also won 680 state legislative seats in a tidal wave that gave Republicans complete control of 25 state legislatures, up from 14; for good measure, they claimed six governorships—boosting their tally to 29 out of 50 states. Among those governorships? Wisconsin, Iowa, Michigan, Ohio, Pennsylvania, and Florida—the very states where GOP-implemented voting restrictions disenfranchised millions of students, people of color, and other key Democratic constituencies.

In other words, those early Tea Party town hall protests were the seeds that grew into today's sorry state of affairs.

THE CHICKENS ARE ROOSTING

In a mirror image of 2010, Resistance protesters are already flooding the town halls of Republican lawmakers across the country. The numbers—and locations—are breathtaking. A thousand protesters booing and jeering Republican representative Chris Stewart in conservative Utah. Representative Marsha Blackburn in Tennessee faced a hostile crowd of hundreds in her safe Republican district. Representative Dave Brat, in the reddest, most remote part of his Trump-voting Virginia district, still faced a storm of heckling as he refused to directly take audience questions. In Representative Tom McClintock's red California district, the congressman fled the angry (but peaceful) crowd, guarded by a police escort. Protesters gleefully captured the cowardly, tough-talking McClintock on video, which became instant viral gold.

After California representative Doug LaMalfa snapped at six hundred constituents at a town hall in Oroville, population 18,000, "You know, you don't yell at church, do you?" constituents shouted back, "Do you lie in church?"

Trump, and his Republican friends, claim those protesters are all a big liberal plot to . . . protest? "The so-called angry crowds in home districts of some Republicans are actually, in numerous cases, planned out by liberal activists. Sad!" tweeted Trump, apparently misunderstanding the fact that *all* activism, even the Tea Party kind, is *planned*. Republicans like Brat also like to claim those protesters are "paid"—perhaps because, in their worldview, people only do things for money, not because the First Amendment guarantees the right to peaceably assemble to petition their representatives.

As one sign in Virginia read, "This grandmother drove 165 miles to be in your grill, Mr. Brat, and no one paid me to be here!"

By the end of March, Indivisible had counted close to three hundred town hall protests organized by its local chapters, with over a hundred thousand estimated participants. Given that many Republican officials chose to hide from their constituents, not all of these events featured a sitting congressperson. But the Resistance is a creative lot, and they made do: In Novi, Michigan, where 200 constituents gathered in a public library for a "David Trott town hall without David Trott" event, a live chicken named Henny Penny stood in for their cowardly representative. The local Indivisible chapter later tweeted, "Interesting fact: Henny Penny the chicken has spent more time with Dave Trott's constituents than the Congressman." Groups like Bernie Sanders' Our Revolution, Planned Parenthood, *Daily Kos*, and others drove tens of thousands more to such events.

Bottom line: when it comes to protests and massive crowds at town halls, more is better! From the Indivisible Guide and other sources, here's what to do:

1. **Join local and national activism groups**; they'll help keep you informed.
2. **Sign up for your elected officials' newsletters.** As Indivisible notes, not only do they sometimes publish their public appearance schedules, but their propaganda also provides insight into their views on key issues.
3. **Call district offices and ask for information on their next town hall**. Be friendly! They don't know if you're friend or foe, no need to tip them off if it's the latter. Ask to be notified whenever any are planned.
4. You can just show up! But you could be more effective if you **coordinate with a local group** (thus making Trump "sad"). Inform them of the event, and get firm commitments to attend.
5. **Prepare several questions in advance.** Make sure your questions are short, fact based, and directly on point. Avoid the desire

to pontificate or ask multiprong questions (which just give the elected official the opportunity to select what she or he wants to answer). Distribute those questions among your group.

6. **Arrive early, meet your group outside the town hall, and get organized.** Remind people to stick to the script. If your group has signs, note that in an oppositional setting, no one with a sign will get to ask questions. So if that's the case, redistribute signs to those who don't intend to speak up.

7. **Grab seats in the front half of the room, but spread out.** As Indivisible says, "This will help reinforce the impression of broad consensus."

8. **When it's time for questions, everyone in your group (without signs) should raise their hands.** Look neutral or friendly to encourage being called on. Stick with the prepared list of questions, and don't let the elected official dodge the question. After you ask your question, your fellow members should applaud to show solidarity. This will also encourage other fellow travelers in the audience to engage on your side. Ask a follow-up if you don't get a direct answer. Others in your group should reinforce your efforts by booing, cheering, clapping, etc. Do not give up the microphone until you get a direct answer. No staffer will physically wrestle the mic away from you. And once you've got your answer, everyone else in the group should raise their hands, lather, rinse, and repeat.

9. **Record everything.** If it's not on video, it didn't happen. After the event, share and post the video anywhere and everywhere you can. Not only are videos a great testament to your own efforts and that of your group, but they give strength and motivation to those planning similar protests elsewhere. And if you're in a red district, even more so! There's nothing more

inspiring than seeing liberals come out proud, and in full force, in conservative territory. You are heroes. Let us applaud you and take strength from your efforts!

10. **Reach out to local media afterward**, offer the video for broadcast, and allow yourself to be a source for any stories about the event.

11. Do this for friendly elected officials too! **Remind our allies in elected office that we have their backs**. Show up to show support and reinforce the good stuff they do.

We've long surrendered the town hall meeting to conservative activists, and they've used our absence from the forum to push America much further to the right than is warranted by their numbers. We can hasten an end to that advantage by engaging in the town hall process. Let's make sure that our elected officials have an accurate accounting of where the energy in their districts (or cities or states) really lives.

5

PROTEST

RECOMMENDED RESOURCES

LaHuelga.com (Spanish)
TheLoyalOpposition.net
ResistanceCalendar.org
ResistanceNearMe.org

ON JANUARY 27, President Steve Bannon and his weak-loser puppet, Donald Trump, issued a travel ban against seven Muslim-majority countries. Chaos immediately erupted at airports around the world as travelers with valid visas were denied entry into the country; even *legal US residents* found themselves caught in the quagmire.

Traveling families, children, businesspeople, musicians, scientists—if they were coming from one of the targeted nations, or even if they just *looked like* they might have, they were treated as criminals, cuffed and herded into holding cells like animals. Customs goons gleefully enforced Bannon's orders.

But then an amazing thing happened: thousands of protesters flooded airports around the country, showing spontaneous solidarity with the victims of Trump's racist, xenophobic policy. They were willing to stand in solidarity and resistance with Muslims, and even *go to airports* to protest their treatment. No one likes to go to airports, even when they *have* to! But for an entire weekend, until several judges struck down Trump's ban, people were willing to be seen and heard, in vivid resistance to Trump's cruelty.

TO CHANGE THE STORYLINE, FIRST . . . SHOW UP

The protests were a direct slap to conventional wisdom, which ordained that "real" Americans should be afraid of and hate Muslims because . . . argle bargle *terrorism*. By targeting Muslim travelers, the Republicans thought they had a winner; surely, Americans want to keep these supposedly hated extremist sympathizers out of the country? Yet in one fell swoop, the protesters annihilated decades of efforts by Right-wing media and the GOP to demonize Islam.

The move certainly played well with the GOP white-supremacist and xenophobic base. But in general, Trumpists don't even have passports, much less live near major international airports in appreciable numbers. By showing up in solidarity, the Resistance changed the storyline. No longer could the lazy media report that Trump was trying to keep us safe by keeping the *bad hombres* out; rather, through powerful images and committed activism, we showcased the clusterfuck that Trump had created and the opposition he had galvanized. We also sent a clear signal to marginalized communities targeted by Trump that the resistance stood in unwavering solidarity with them.

Much in the same way, the Women's March galvanized the Resistance and created the first major catalyst for organizing just one day after

Trump's sparsely attended inauguration. But the march wasn't effective because of the half million protesters who converged on Washington, DC (as impactful as that was). It worked because of the thousands of satellite events. Organizers expected 80,000 in Los Angeles; they got 750,000 instead. Over 100,000 marched in Denver, another 100,000 in Portland, Oregon, and 60,000 in Houston.

THE WOMEN'S MARCH WAS THE SINGLE LARGEST PROTEST IN AMERICAN HISTORY, WITH AT LEAST FOUR MILLION TAKING TO THE STREETS.

But those are all big Democratic cities. Perhaps more exciting were the 30 who marched in Stanley, Idaho—population 69. Or the 500 who marched in Vermillion, South Dakota, population 10,571. Or the 400 who marched in Cody, Wyoming, population 9,833.

Collectively, the Women's March was the single largest protest in American history, with at least four million taking to the streets. And while conservatives shrug off big-city protests, pretending they never happened, it was harder to do so when people were marching in Tulsa, Oklahoma, or Topeka, Kansas. It was hard for fake news to claim a sweeping presidential mandate for Trump when conservatives saw, with their own eyes, the massive discontent in their own backyards.

Protesting is powerful. But not all protests are created equal. There's a trick to effective protest, and it hinges around making sure that the purpose of the protest is clear. The Resistance will need to protest often, so we may as well get good at it:

1. **Be patriotic; fly a flag or wear a flag pin.** The Resistance represents the American ideal, as captured in those words written on the Statue of Liberty: "Give me your tired, your poor, / Your

huddled masses yearning to breathe free." We also are the natural heirs to the foundational notion, put forth in the Declaration of Independence, that "all men are created equal." We are America, so no need to cede the flag to conservatives who hate us for our freedoms.

2. **Signs are fun!** Protests are, in many ways, a party. And what better way to share your joy, your passion, or your anger than by clever, creative signs? Go and look at social media shares of protests, and then note how many of them are really of people's signs. A clever sign just begs to go viral.

3. **Stay on point.** Liberal protests have traditionally been unfocused, with myriad competing and unrelated issues and groups all vying to make *their* message the dominant one. In the end, *everyone's* message gets lost in the cacophony. The purpose of the Women's March was singular and clear, as was that of the airport protests and the science march. You want the narrative to be "thousands marched in opposition/support of X," not "a thousand people marched for no clear reason." The march itself should never be the headline; the *purpose* should be.

4. **Stay nonviolent.** This should go without saying, but there's a segment of the far anarchist left that uses peaceful protests as cover for their own violent behavior. If the goal of a protest is to highlight opposition or support for an issue, nothing will destroy that effort faster than having violence become the story. That doesn't just mean behaving oneself and practicing nonviolent resistance, but also helping keep the peace at protests to keep destructive elements at bay.

5. **Be novel and different.** "A bunch of people marched downtown" is a boring story and will get little pickup in any media outlet, whether social or traditional. So don't do the obvious.

Shake things up. Cheering Muslim travelers as they (finally) emerged through customs? Tearjerker! Media gold! Two thousand protesters participating in the Women's March in Fairbanks, Alaska, in *subzero* temperatures? Whoa, that's inspiring! And any time protesters can get in Trump's face (looking at you jealously, West Palm Beach), that is *always* perfect, because anything that directly enrages Trump is gold.

The steady stream of anti-Trump protests has had another key effect: it has stiffened the spines of squishy Democrats. We've always complained of a weak Democratic Party, and yes, it's been generally true! But put yourself in their shoes—relentlessly attacked by Tea Party conservatives and the dominant conservative media, with little coordinated effort on our side to push back and show support. Our relative absence from the political battlefield made it easier for some Democrats to cave to conservatives and move to the right than to do the correct thing. The squeaky wheel gets the oil, after all.

By emerging from the shadows and being present, engaged, and active, the Resistance has given Democrats ample backup and plenty of reasons to stiffen their resolve. That's why most Democrats, including several red-state senators, stuck together to filibuster the Supreme Court nomination of Neil Gorsuch—something that likely wouldn't have happened even a year ago. If we have their backs, it makes it easier for them to have *our* backs. Pretty obvious, right?

The Resistance movement is real, like a wave. Elected Democrats have two choices: either they ride that wave and take it wherever the energy goes, or they get swept out of the way. It took many DC Democrats some time to adjust; some never will. But as a party, we're well on our way to moving the whole thing leftward, into that "resistance" orientation. Our future looks bright.

So protest to remind America that Trump, his party, and his policies are unacceptable to a no-longer-silent majority. Protest to have fun in a time of darkness, and to connect with like-minded people who share a common goal. And protest to give Democrats a reason to stand firm and fight hard. The Resistance is already working—keep it up!

6

JOIN INDIVISIBLE

RECOMMENDED RESOURCES
IndivisibleGuide.com

WE'VE BEEN BORROWING heavily from Indivisible, so here's your next action: join Indivisible! Seriously, just go do it. There are already thousands of chapters around the country, in every state. If there isn't a chapter near you, start one! The Indivisible Guide has practical step-by-step instructions on how to do so.

Note that each group is independent, making the organization a truly distributed grassroots bottom-up operation. As they explain, "Groups in our directory are wholly independent; they are listed provided they agree to resist Trump's agenda, focus on local, defensive congressional advocacy, and embrace progressive values." Indivisible provides some focus and direction, but what makes these groups truly exciting is that they are building the local infrastructure we need to have a real fifty-state movement.

So that's it! Sometimes, some of the most effective actions are also some of the simplest. Join Indivisible now.

JOIN *DAILY KOS*

RECOMMENDED RESOURCES

DailyKos.com

DAILY KOS IS committed to electing more and better Democrats. It is, at its core, a partisan site, seeking to influence our nation's politics through the electoral process by helping progressives across the spectrum connect with, debate, coordinate with, activate, and learn from each other.

Markos launched *Daily Kos* in 2002 primarily as a personal vehicle to vent against the injustices of the last Republican disaster, President Dick Cheney, and his White House minion George W. Bush. If you think there is a dearth of genuinely liberal voices in the media today, you should go back and check the history of the lead-up to the Iraq War—it was desperate: the *New York Times* itself was the lead cheerleader for the war, publishing story after bogus story about "weapons of mass destruction" by Judith Miller (surprising no one, Miller would eventually leave the *Times* to become a Fox News and right-wing media personality). This theme of bad "neutral" reporting repeated itself across the broad spectrum of mainstream media, and forget about any explicitly liberal voices.

Over at *Time* magazine (which was still a thing people cared about back then) the one liberal columnist, Joe Klein, wagged his fingers at liberals on TV, saying, "Sooner or later, this guy has to be taken out. Saddam has—Saddam Hussein has to be taken out." The biggest liberal voice on TV was Alan Colmes, the designated liberal punching bag for Sean Hannity on Fox News. Phil Donahue lost his MSNBC show because he was a "difficult public face for NBC in a time of war," providing "a home for the liberal antiwar agenda at the same time that our competitors are waving the flag at every opportunity."

DAILY KOS FOCUSES ON PRODUCING ACTIONABLE NEWS—AND THEN GIVES YOU THE ACTIONS THAT ADVANCE THE CAUSE.

Given the political and media environment at the time, it wasn't long before Markos' blog had attracted thousands of like-minded "pragmatic progressives" who found solace and sanity—and the ability to post their own musings—on *Daily Kos*. From those humble beginnings, *Daily Kos* grew to become the largest partisan liberal media outlet in the country; by the end of 2016, the site had over twenty million unique visitors during peak months, an email action list over three million strong, and over a million followers on Facebook. In the last six years, the *Daily Kos* community raised over $50 million for candidates and allied organizations. Most recently, *Daily Kos* raised close to $2 million for Jon Ossoff in a House special election in suburban Atlanta's Sixth Congressional District.

BOOTS ON THE GROUND, ACTUALLY

Prior to his career as a political entrepreneur and activist, Markos served as an artillery fire direction specialist in the US Army (where his nickname "Kos" originated) and was on active duty during the first Gulf War. His knowledge of military logistics positioned him as an informed voice of opposition to the Iraq War and made it difficult to paint him as an unpatriotic traitor: unlike most of his critics in the Republican Right, Markos had actually served his nation in uniform. He had worn army-issued combat boots.

Markos' military experience also translated well into the political realm, where only fighters win. To this day, too many liberals think politics is icky, and partisan politics . . . even ickier. They think themselves intellectually superior for depending on the "neutral" *New York Times* or NPR for their news, unlike those uncouth conservatives, who are spoon-fed Koch brothers' talking points on Rush Limbaugh and Fox News.

But the problem with media bias isn't that the *Times* is insufficiently liberal; it's that liberals still think the *Times* is on "our side." That's not the *Times'* job. Whether they succeed or not, their job is to report the news. Fox News, Breitbart, and Rush Limbaugh? Their job is to make sure Republicans *win.*

And that's what *Daily Kos* is and always has been: a hub for liberal news and activism focused on helping our side win. That doesn't mean the site engages in fake news. Why would they need to? As Stephen Colbert famously said, "Reality has a well-known liberal bias." As such, *Daily Kos* focuses on producing *actionable* news—and then gives you the actions that advance the cause.

As a full-suite political media operation, *Daily Kos* offers several ways for you to engage, and they're all easy:

1. **Join the *Daily Kos* action list.** You'll receive both a daily digest of the most viral stories on *Daily Kos* that day, actions focused on the issues you care most about, and events in your local area.
2. **Friend *Daily Kos* on Facebook.** Same as above. If you get your news from Facebook, make sure *Daily Kos* is in your feed.
3. **Read *Daily Kos* regularly.** *Daily Kos* has among the best political coverage, whether partisan or otherwise. Every day, hundreds of stories are posted, both from staff writers and from its community members. Because of the site's extensive local reach—there are over 3,000 regular contributors—*Daily Kos* readers are among the most informed citizens.
4. **Join *Daily Kos*.** Create an account! That allows you to recommend your favorite stories and comments, write comments and stories, and keep better track of comment threads by marking comments you've already read.
5. **Write comments.** Join the conversation! Sure, it's politics, so people disagree, and it's the Internet, so sometimes people are—gasp!—wrong. But there are also thousands of smart, well-informed, funny, and insightful commenters, all of whom add a great deal to any discussion on the site. In addition, entire subcommunities live on the site, from book lovers to support groups for quitting smoking to expat Dems. When you have this many people gathering in a single place, amazing things happen.
6. **Write stories.** *Daily Kos* is a self-serve blogging platform. Instead of thinking, "Why doesn't someone cover my issue?," cover it yourself! Write about the issues that motivate you,

about the injustices that infuriate you, about the great event you just attended (maybe even a town hall!) or that local race everyone should pay attention to.

There is nothing like *Daily Kos*, anywhere: it's a news and information site, an activism hub, and an online community. As CQ Roll Call columnist Patricia Murphy wrote in April 2017, on the eve of that Georgia special election, "The one thing we can take away from the 6th District special election, no matter who wins, is that *Daily Kos* put John Ossoff on the map for national Democrats looking for a way to fight back against Donald Trump. And after fading into the background of progressive politics for the last few cycles, *Daily Kos* has made themselves an undeniable force in the resistance to Trump's America."

We all know the importance of the right-wing media machine to their electoral success. You can be part of growing what is already the Left's largest media outlet.

8

READ
RULES FOR RADICALS

RECOMMENDED RESOURCES
Rules for Radicals by Saul Alinsky

IN 1972, longtime community organizer Saul Alinsky, in an interview with *Playboy* magazine, fretted about losing the white middle class to reactionary forces.

"The middle class actually feels more defeated and lost today on a wide range of issues than the poor do," he said—almost as if he had a time machine and had seen what the future foretold. He went on:

> *The situation is supercharged with both opportunity and danger. There's a second revolution seething beneath the*

surface of middle-class America—the revolution of a bewildered, frightened and as-yet-inarticulate group of desperate people groping for alternatives—for hope. Their fears and their frustrations over their impotence can turn into political paranoia and demonize them, driving them to the right, making them ripe for the plucking by some guy on horseback promising a return to the vanished verities of yesterday.

Alinsky didn't just foresee the rise of Ronald Reagan; he anticipated the reactionary Right's conquest of today's Republican Party. "The right would give them scapegoats for their misery—blacks, hippies, Communists—and if it wins, this country will become the first totalitarian state with a national anthem celebrating 'the land of the free and the home of the brave.'"

Shortly after giving the interview, Alinsky died of a heart attack, but not before cementing his legacy as a progressive organizer in his seminal book, *Rules for Radicals,* published in 1971. The book details lessons learned from Alinsky's thirty-one years of activism, mostly in poor and blighted neighborhoods in Chicago (and then California, New York, Michigan, and elsewhere). Conservatives, to this day, view Alinsky with a mixture of awe and fury. The conservative *Weekly Standard*'s William F. Buckley once called him "very close to being an organizational genius." Former Republican House leader Dick Armey gave copies of *Rules for Radicals* to members of the Tea Party group he headed, FreedomWorks.

FORMER REPUBLICAN HOUSE LEADER DICK ARMEY GAVE COPIES OF *RULES FOR RADICALS* TO MEMBERS OF THE TEA PARTY GROUP HE HEADED, FREEDOMWORKS.

Meanwhile, conservatives continue to attack Democrats for supposed ties to the late activist. Hillary Clinton based her honors thesis on Alinsky's work (and in fact interviewed him several times for the project), while Barack Obama was a community organizer in Chicago's South Side, working with activists schooled in Alinsky tactics.

What is it about Alinsky that is so threatening to the Republican establishment—so much so that they co-opted his messaging (though definitely not his values)? It was his belief in empowering marginalized communities of color. (He would later embrace doing the same with marginalized middle-class whites.) One Breitbart author questioned "what role Mr. Alinsky's writings and overthrow tactics have had on [Obama]. (By 'overthrow tactics' I mean Alinsky's methods for not only persuading but also enabling the 'have-nots' in our society to overthrow the haves and take away their power.)"

Conservatives certainly don't want any "have-nots" taking away the power of any "haves"; their entire theory of governance is predicated on punishing the impoverished and rewarding the rich and privileged. Just witness the popular-vote loser Donald Trump. After pandering to poor whites to win the election, he quickly proposed policies that would devastate rural working-class whites, while at the same time stocking his cabinet with a record number of billionaires and Wall Street tycoons.

While the activist tool set is different today than it was back in the decidedly analog seventies, Alinsky's broader themes remain just as relevant today. Some key rules:

"POWER IS NOT ONLY WHAT YOU HAVE BUT WHAT THE ENEMY THINKS YOU HAVE."

Power is derived from two main sources—money and people. "Have-nots" must build power from flesh and blood.

We cannot match the Koch brothers' wealth, or that of Mitt Romney, or Donald Trump, or Sheldon Adelson, or Pete Peterson; the combined wealth of the GOP's upper-crust patrons is larger than the GDP of most small countries. What we do have is more people. Anything that demonstrates an army of supporters is helpful, whether it's thousands marching in the streets or thousands signing an online petition.

"MAKE THE ENEMY LIVE UP TO THEIR OWN BOOK OF RULES."

If the rule is that every letter gets a reply, send thirty thousand letters. You can kill them with this because no one can possibly obey all of their own rules.

When Trump lobbed $70 million in cruise missiles into Syria, he did so without congressional oversight or approval. Immediately, Twitter was inundated with retweets of multiple old Trump tweets where he demanded Obama stay out of Syria and warning him that any action would require congressional approval. This has become a fun tactic—Trump does something, and people then dig up old tweets of him saying the exact opposite. In fact, this happens so often that one person tweeted, "I swear if Trump randomly, like, tripped on a squirrel or something we'd find an old tweet of his saying only fat losers trip on squirrels."

Pointing out Trump's hypocrisy might not be the most impactful action, but it chips away at his credibility. And if it makes him gun-shy on Twitter, it removes one of his most potent weapons.

Similarly, note how earlier in this book, we talked about Republican congressional offices being so overwhelmed with calls that they couldn't get their regular work done. They couldn't ignore those calls! Since we don't *want* them to get any regular work done, mission accomplished! Anything that stymies, delays, obstructs, or blocks Republicans is a win.

"RIDICULE IS MAN'S MOST POTENT WEAPON."

There is no defense. It's irrational. It's infuriating. It also works as a key pressure point to force the enemy into concessions.

Trump is angry when people refer to "President Bannon." Trump is angry when Melissa McCarthy plays Trump press secretary Sean Spicer on *Saturday Night Live*. Trump is angry when people laugh at his meager inauguration crowd sizes. Trump is really, *really* angry when people point to his tiny, microscopic hands. In fact, given his outsize ego, utter lack of self-esteem, and tendency to absurd bravado, Trump may be the easiest person to ridicule in political history. He doesn't want to be a loser, he doesn't want people pointing out he's a loser. And people who get ridiculed are losers.

So not only does such ridicule knock Trump off his game, but it continuously prevents people from normalizing him. His tantrums confirm the worst criticisms against him—that he is thin-skinned, irrational, and obsessed with self-image over substance. By sticking by such a clown, every Republican and conservative also becomes a ripe target for ridicule. Plus, ridicule is fun! And the more fun we have, the easier it will be to maintain morale and energy in the Resistance.

THE MORE FUN WE HAVE, THE EASIER IT WILL
BE TO MAINTAIN MORALE AND ENERGY IN
THE RESISTANCE.

"A GOOD TACTIC IS ONE THAT YOUR PEOPLE ENJOY."

They'll keep doing it without urging and come back to do more. They're doing their thing, and will even suggest better ones.

It's worth repeating the importance of finding meaningful actions that are both impactful and fun. Yes, saving our democracy is serious stuff. But relentless earnestness won't sustain activism over the long haul. Fight hard, but have fun doing so.

"A TACTIC THAT DRAGS ON TOO LONG BECOMES A DRAG."

Don't become old news.

"Old news" really means "ignored." The point of activism is to have an impact. Off the launching pad, the Occupy movement had a great deal of impact. Wielding its powerful "99 percent" meme, it began a real conversation about income inequality that continues to this day. But over the subsequent months, it became less about income inequality and more about squatting in public areas. The tactic wore out its welcome, but its adherents refused to let it go. Their refusal to adapt and engage in electoral policy (unlike the Tea Party) sealed their fate. Today, no one talks about the Occupy movement.

"KEEP THE PRESSURE ON."

Keep trying new things to keep the opposition off balance. As the opposition masters one approach, hit them from the flank with something new.

On day two of the Trump regime, millions of Americans marched in the streets. A couple of weeks later, they were occupying airports to protest the Muslim ban. Then a barrage of phone calls to congressional offices scuttled the GOP's first attempt to repeal Obamacare. Meanwhile, it turned out that referring to "President Bannon" *was* getting under Trump's skin, and Bannon's Svengali job was in jeopardy. Republicans are actively avoiding public, town-hall-style events for fear of facing protesters. If there's one thing the Resistance is getting right from the start, it's relentlessly pressuring Republicans anywhere and everywhere they rear their ugly heads. It's got them disoriented, off balance, and nervous. And it's when people are under such pressure that they start making mistakes.

As timely today as it was in 1971, *Rules for Radicals* is a must-read for every Resistance fighter.

9

MEATSPACE TRUMPS VIRTUAL ORGANIZING

RECOMMENDED RESOURCES

5Calls.org
CivicDinners.com
MoveOn.org
OurRevolution.com

LIVING IN THE digital age has made it infinitely easier to organize online. But digital relationships are no substitute for the power of gathering people physically together. Humans are social creatures, and we take strength from coming together for a shared cause. Our brains are wired for social interaction; we evolved in the physical presence of social groups, and despite the amount of time we spend staring at a screen, we still need human contact to survive and thrive.

"Oxytocin—known as the 'love hormone' because of its important role in the formation and maintenance of mother-child bonding and sexual attachments—is actually involved in a much broader range of social connections," reported *Psychology Today* in September 2013, on a breakthrough Stanford University School of Medicine study. "The researchers discovered that oxytocin released through any type of social connectivity triggered the release of serotonin. In a chain reaction, the serotonin then activated the 'reward circuitry' of the nucleus accumbens resulting in a happy feeling." That's the same brain chemistry that gives us the "runner's high" and creates the effects from drugs like LSD and MDMA.

Antidepressants work to regulate serotonin levels in the body, which in depressed people are out of whack. Prisoners in solitary confinement literally suffer brain damage from lack of social interaction. The opposite of solitary confinement, more social interaction, actually makes people work better: A Bank of America call center changed from staggered coffee breaks to one big communal one. The result, according to an MIT study of the experiment? Fifteen million dollars in productivity gains. It turns out that staff would share work tips, leading to smarter employees. Gossip actually improved productivity!

People are more effective when they work together, *in person*. That's why protests are so personally validating, whether you're marching down the Mall in Washington, DC, or your local city square, or attending a congressional town hall. This is why megachurches are such a critical component of conservative political organizing: they provide a physical space for people to establish deep connections and a shared sense of identity. It is in such settings that we forge the individual connections that build community.

People are quicker to trust one another after in-person meetings; they inspire positive feelings and build lasting relationships that can then extend more easily into the virtual realm. In-person meetings allow us to read people's body language (which is basically impossible to do online), see what excites them and what doesn't, and adjust our interactions on the fly to show empathy and understanding—which is crucial when looking for volunteers or getting a shy person to share a story.

So yes, the science confirms what we already knew. So how can you help bring people together to meet face-to-face?

1. **Provide organizing space.** If you have space in your home or business for people to gather, offer it to local organizing groups. If you have a relationship with a local coffee shop, church, art gallery, or performance space, help make it available.

2. **Host a phone-banking event.** Various organizations have virtual phone-banking applications. Get a bunch of your friends together to make calls on behalf of candidates or allies.

3. **Host a movie night.** Gather people around a documentary or political event, like a State of the Union address, debate, or major speech, educating and building community at the same time.

4. **Host a fundraiser.** There are an endless number of candidates and organizations that could use support. And in this blossoming age of small-dollar donors, even small amounts add up to big amounts when thousands participate.

5. **Offer home base before a vigil or protest.** Ready to head out to a big event? Gather people for an informal social before heading out.

6. **Host a conversation.** The organization Civic Dinners gives you a step-by-step guide on how to gather people for intimate civic discussions. Use their suggested topics or come up with your own.

7. **Host a game night.** Gather your local activists and build community the fun way—by having fun! Politics can't always be earnest struggle. The more fun it is for people, the deeper the social connections become, the more engaged everyone will remain. And remember, we're in this fight for the long haul.

While much of the Resistance will be organized online, the strongest, most effective connections and impact will take place offline. Be a connector, providing time and space for Resistance fighters to gather, plot, and act.

PROTECT YOUR PRIVACY

RECOMMENDED RESOURCES

1password.com
ConstitutionalCommunications.org
DuckDuckGo Search Engine
EqualityLabs.org
LastPass.com
Slack.com
Tor Browser
TwoFactorAuth.org
WhisperSystems.org

BUMBLING, BUFFOONISH Donald Trump poses many threats to our nation. Among them is the assault on our privacy.

Shortly after taking office, Trump called for a boycott of Apple after the iPhone maker refused to install a "back door"—a secret entryway law enforcement and intelligence agencies could use to peer into your private communications. (It failed. *Loser.*) He has advocated closing "certain areas" of the Internet (as if that's even technically possible) and dismissed free speech concerns out of hand: "Somebody will say, 'Oh freedom of speech, freedom of speech.' These are foolish people. We have a lot of foolish people."

Needless to say, Trump's attorney general, Jeff Sessions, is no champion of civil rights himself. As America's "top cop," Sessions is fully on board with the assault on our liberties: during his confirmation hearings, he said, "It is also critical . . . that national security and criminal investigators be able to overcome encryption."

Meanwhile, Trump had (and potentially still has—we may never know!) Russia's foreign intelligence apparatus operating on his behalf. So not only does Trump control his own domestic secret police force, but Trump-friendly hackers have the ability, means, and desire to electronically damage his opponents, like the hacks into the Democratic National Committee.

DON'T CLICK! AND OTHER TRICKS

The scary truth is that the more effective your activism and that of your Resistance allies, the greater the risk that you will be targeted by hostile hackers. So it's imperative, particularly in this digital era, to protect yourself to the best of your abilities.

1. **Be careful which links you click in your emails.** Russian hackers broke into the Democratic National Committee via an email spoof link, fooling Clinton campaign chairman John Podesta into giving them access to his account. No matter how strong your personal security measures, nothing can protect you if you fall for one of those tricks. So how do you know if a link

is dangerous? Hover or mouse over the link and take a look at the URL it's sending you to. If it's a shortened link (like to TinyURL.com), don't click on it. If it's a misspelled version of a legitimate website (like "Gooogle.com"), don't click on it. If it has a top-level domain that looks sketchy (the letters after the "dot" in a URL, like "Google.biz"), don't click on it. And really listen to your inner warning system; if anything seems off or weird, don't click. Period. In this case, it's good to be paranoid.

2. **Move your group's internal deliberations to a secure communications tool.** There are better ways to communicate and organize than email, with all its inherent flaws. Slack is a stellar collaboration tool (make sure to set settings to delete messages after a certain period of time, say, two weeks or a month). Signal allows encrypted text messaging and voice calls between users and is a favorite tool of cryptographers.

3. **Do not open attachments from unknown sources.** Unless you know the sender and you are expecting a file, do not click on attachments. If you want to open an attachment but are unsure of its safety, open the file in Google Drive, which provides separation between the file (and any malicious code it might contain) and your computer or device.

4. **Use a six-digit passcode to unlock your devices.** Law enforcement can compel you to use your thumb to unlock your phone. They cannot force you to give them your phone's passcode. Aside from the legal absurdity, someone can unlock your phone if you're unconscious. So yes, it sucks to surrender the convenience of thumbprint recognition. But unless you're ready to surrender the content of your phone to some Trump goon, like the customs officials demanding access to travelers' social media accounts at airports, take the extra precaution. (Bonus: you'll be

less likely to be tempted to unlock your phone while driving, which could save your or someone else's life.) Using six-digit combinations creates a million possible variations—far more secure than with four digits, which offers ten thousand possible combinations.

5. **Enable two-factor authentication.** Two-factor authentication adds an extra layer of security to your online accounts by requiring an additional confirmation when you log in from a new device, usually via text message (but also via voice call, hardware token, or software). That means a hacker can't access your account merely with your log-in and password. So, for example, the first time you log in to Gmail from a new computer, Google can ask you to input a six-digit code sent to you via text or voice call to verify that it is in fact you who is trying to log in.

6. **Use better passwords, and use a password manager.** For all that's good and holy, please stop with the easy-to-guess passwords! So nothing with your birthday, or your child's name, or "12345678," or "password." You don't want to be the password bum who gives a hostile force access to your group's communications (not to mention your own private financial life). Do not reuse passwords. The more random the password, the better. Password managers can generate the most secure passwords and spare you the hassle of trying to remember them across multiple devices. 1Password and LastPass are both great for these purposes.

7. **Careful what you download, and always update software.** Immediately after Trump's inauguration, Ivanka Trump tweeted out a link to an app, saying, "Confront your fear of flying with this turbulence-predicting app." Trump-loving people downloaded the app in droves. According to BuzzFeed,

the app—which tracks user locations—was developed by people with close ties to the Russian government. Some security experts even claimed it was a Russian intelligence operation. So if nothing else, don't allow apps to track your location unless you absolutely trust the app and need the tracking (like Google Maps). Meanwhile, make sure all your apps and devices are up-to-date, as updates often contain patches to security holes.

8. **Block your forward-facing cameras.** Hackers can access your device cameras and headphones to keep tabs on you. (Even a school district in suburban Philadelphia got busted spying on its students through their school-issued computers.) Put a strip of tape, Post-it note, or sticker over the camera whenever you're not using it. Also, unplug your headphones when not using them, as even those are hackable and can be used to spy on you.

9. **And more . . .** Make sure your computer's hard drive is encrypted. You can easily find instructions on how to do it by googling your operating system and version. Download the Tor browser, which anonymizes your browsing activities, for sensitive searches. If you'd like to search without leaving a paper trail for others to read, try the DuckDuckGo.com search engine. When signing up to sites or services online, don't use your real email address or phone number. You can get a throwaway email account anywhere, and get a different phone number from Google Voice.

Security always requires a tradeoff between safety and convenience, and none of the steps above are convenient. But there is value in surrendering some of that convenience—you will make it harder for hostile forces to undermine you and your fellow activists, interfere in your personal life, and otherwise hamper your efforts with the Resistance.

11

PUT YOUR MONEY WHERE YOUR VALUES ARE

RECOMMENDED RESOURCES

Buycott.com
CallTrump.How
DemocraticCoalition.org
GrabYourWallet.org
InjusticeBoycott.com

IN OUR CASE for the popular-vote loser Donald Trump's impeachment, we noted his illegal profiteering from the White House; we also noted that Republicans are utterly disinterested in upholding the law.

Meanwhile, there will be companies that try to profit from Trump's policies. When New York taxi drivers refused to serve local airports in support of the Muslim ban protests, Uber tried to profit, removing

THE RESISTANCE HANDBOOK: 45 WAYS TO FIGHT TRUMP

surge pricing from trips from those airports. For-profit private prison stock prices surged 100 percent after Trump's inauguration. Stock prices for military-industrial complex companies similarly skyrocketed, with investors anticipating the wars Trump would likely bring them.

So if Republicans and certain corporations won't fight for our Constitution, it's up to us to do so. And when it comes to Trump's business interests and those of his allies, we can certainly do our part to undermine their economic interests—starting with our wallets.

1. **Avoid anything with the Trump brand.** The Trump family's narcissism helps us out quite a bit here. They slap their names on most of their products, making them particularly easy to avoid. But they're also increasingly aware of the toxicity of their brand. They are launching a new hotel brand named Scion. And Ivanka Trump merchandise was seen rebranded as Adrienne Vittadini at at least one retailer. Keep an eye out for efforts to mask their business dealings.

2. **Call Trump businesses to complain about Trump.** CallTrump.how will give you random Trump properties to call with your concerns about the president. He's their boss, and he refuses to fully divest himself of his businesses while in power. So however you can get the message to his people is fair game.

3. **Boycott businesses that support Trump.** GrabYourWallet .org has a regularly compiled list of companies to boycott, such as L.L.Bean, whose heiress and board member Linda Bean is a generous contributor to Trump, and New Balance, whose CEO donated nearly $400,000 to Trump's election effort; there are also retailers like Macy's and Zappos who carry Trumpfamily-branded merchandise. Download the Boycott Trump

app for your devices. And make sure you let those companies know that 1) you are boycotting them, and 2) why.

4. **Support companies that oppose Trump.** Nordstrom's stock price *climbed* after they decided to drop Ivanka Trump's merchandise. Starbucks has promised to hire thousands of refugees in direct response to Trump's immigration rhetoric. Shoes.com dropped Ivanka's line of shoes in response to a Twitter campaign, declaring that those shoes weren't selling well anyway (adding insult to injury is always a nice touch!).

After Uber's disgraceful strikebreaking efforts, over two hundred thousand people deleted the app from their devices as part of the #DeleteUber campaign. That may be a small percentage of its (claimed) forty million users, but the PR hit stung, particularly as it remains embroiled in a series of scandals that have hobbled the company. As a result of the boycott, Uber CEO Travis Kalanick quit a Trump advisory panel he served on, giving Trump one less stooge in corporate America to lend credibility to his illegitimate regime.

An early 2017 market survey by Simmons Research found that 34 percent of Americans would prefer not to buy products from a Trump-supporting company, or a company with a Trump-supporting CEO. Thirty percent said they would pay more for a competitor's product. Even 23 percent of *Republicans* would avoid a Trump-supporting company. By turning up the heat on these companies and CEOs, we can isolate and ostracize Trump.

THE SCIENCE OF BRAND CAMPAIGNS

According to research by Brayden King at Northwestern's Kellogg School of Management, if a boycott receives national attention (about

25 percent do), a company will take action—even if sales aren't affected. From a corporate perspective, that makes sense: Early in a boycott, there's no way to know how customer relationships, brand values, and sales might be impacted. Unless you are the Koch brothers and don't give a damn, it's oftentimes easier—and almost always less costly—to respond responsibly to the boycott, make concessions, and protect the bottom line. "Companies realize boycotts are not troublesome because [of] sales—they worry about the media attention they create," King told the *Atlantic*. In the age of social media, "national attention" has become as easy as a few clicks. So let's add to our list:

5. **Promote information about anti-Trump product boycotts.**
   Share that information on social media, helping build the kind of national awareness that makes many companies cry "uncle."
   A company has more than sales to worry about. It has to protect its brand—a damaged brand can hamper long-term growth prospects, particularly with the fastest-growing market segments: people of color, millennials, and women (i.e., not old, conservative white men). It also has to attract the best employees, something that companies like, say, Uber can have a hard time doing when under a dark cloud. It can give impetus to competitors, either to enter a market, sensing a wounded incumbent, or give also-rans a new lease on life—witness Lyft's recent growth spurt on the back of Uber's PR nightmares (Lyft, by the way, isn't run by assholes and treats its drivers well).

Finally, remember that Trump isn't the only problem we face, it's the entire Republican Party. So . . .

6. **All of the above applies to conservative brands, companies, and business supporters.** We need to make sure that if companies support conservative causes, consumers will make decisions based on that support.

Of course, conservatives, like liberals, have the same First Amendment right to say almost anything they want. However, they don't have a First Amendment right to keep their sponsors, customers, audience, or supporters. Actions have consequences, and we, as consumers, have the right to spend our time and money at places that align with our values. And if the likes of Donald Trump or Bill O'Reilly don't align with our values? Then we let the free market speak and take our money elsewhere.

PROTECT THE CULTURE

1 2

IT'S OUR FLAG— OWN IT!

RECOMMENDED RESOURCES

WhatMakesAmericaGreat.us

THE STARS AND Stripes is our flag. It is the physical symbol and embodiment of progressive values.

Ours is an America where we celebrate the First Amendment by voicing our opposition to the Trump regime, peacefully assembling and petitioning the government for a redress of grievances.

Ours is an America where people of all colors and backgrounds gathered at airports in support of Muslims targeted by Trump's travel ban, cheering hijab-wearing travelers as they emerged from customs—just fifteen miles from Ellis Island and the Statue of Liberty—and were reunited with their families.

Ours is an America where any two adult humans who love each other can get legally married.

Ours is an America where the American Islamic community raised money to repair damage at Jewish cemeteries around the country while Trump and his racist regime—staffed by white nationalists and self-proclaimed Nazis *in the White House*—"committed grotesque acts and omissions reflecting anti-Semitism" according to the Anne Frank Center for Mutual Respect. "A cancer of anti-Semitism [has] infected his own administration," they added.

Ours is an America where the oil, coal, and fracking industries have to follow the rules to keep our air and water clean and our children's health safe—or get shut down by public health regulators.

Ours is an America where large numbers of whites and Latinos and Asians support the Black Lives Matter movement, and their perfectly reasonable demands for the police to stop killing people in cold blood, in the streets.

Ours is an America that is successfully resisting efforts to discriminate against transgendered citizens by denying them the right to use public bathrooms.

Our is an America where people don't die from lack of health insurance, and where people can retire and age in dignity, not in poverty.

Ours is an America where women are equal members of society and aren't penalized for having ovaries, either in the workplace or at the doctor's office.

None of this should be controversial, and if you're a *real American*, it's not. Basic human decency, respect for your neighbors, and belief in the freedom to *be yourself* and the right to *control your own body* are at the core of our nation's DNA. We have plenty of work to do to fulfill our promises and to fully live up to our ideals—but with dedicated Resistance fighters and some focused, committed political organizing, we'll get there.

So own and embrace America's patriotic symbols, starting with the flag. Talk to people about how great *our* America is, and how much better it will be if we continue organizing and fighting for it.

As long as we're building the infrastructure we need to defeat Republican conservatism, we may as well make clear that we're doing it out of a passionate love of our country and its ideals. What's more patriotic than that?

THROUGH THE CONSERVATIVE LOOKING GLASS

Contrasted with the values that underpin liberalism, conservative America is . . . downright weird. Thanks to the reality-distortion effect of Fox News and right-wing media, in the Republican mind, America is a place where people should look at their non-white, non-English-speaking, non-straight, non-cisgender neighbors with distrust and fear, and assume jealously that "other" people (who usually seem to have brown skin, weirdly enough) are stealing their hard-earned tax dollars.

Republican America pretends to be individualistic, a place where everyone pulls themselves up by their own bootstraps—even though most red states suck resources from most blue states, and rural areas suck resources from the cities. It's an America where freedom of religion is replaced with state-sanctioned Christian theocracy, and where the libertine morality of liberalism is a threat to the conservative Christian ideals that Republicans claim are embedded in our Constitution. It is a nation where mythical hordes of "illegals" murder and pillage innocent women and children, one in which police are under siege from "thugs" from the

Black Lives Matter movement, and in which women are an emasculating force, preventing "real men from being men" (in other words, rapey and misogynist). It is an America where ISIS is hiding under our beds, and our military is too underfunded (thanks, Obama!) to do anything about it.

Don't ask conservatives to be consistent—their mantra of "America, fuck yeah!" is clearly at odds with the constant portrayal of a nation in decline. "If we don't get tough, and if we don't get smart, and fast, we're not going to have our country anymore," Trump said at one campaign event. "There will be nothing, absolutely nothing, left."

In reality, in 2016, border crossings by undocumented immigrants were plummeting, violent crimes continued their three-decade decline, ISIS was losing ground in both Syria and Iraq, and the abortion rate was at the lowest point since *Roe v. Wade*—half that of 1980, thanks almost entirely to the Obama policy of providing easier access to free contraception (another thing conservatives find abhorrent). Under Obama's administration, 11.3 million jobs were created, and despite his being accused of being a communist, capitalism and the stock market soared high. Now, issues of income inequality and underemployment festered, so not all was sunny, but given an obstructionist Congress and relentless conservative attacks, the progress we had (and there *was* progress) was substantial.

So if conservatives hate and fear the real America so much, they don't deserve to wave the American flag. They have corrupted the ideals it represents—a land where political, religious, and economic outcasts can come together to build something new, where all people are seen and treated as equals, and where everyone has an inalienable right to life, liberty, and the pursuit of happiness.

These core, foundational American values are now inarguably liberal values. And while our nation often fails to live up to those values, our shifting demographics will better position us to build this new America, one in which we respect the dignity of the individual, while working together for the collective good of society.

So wear a flag pin! Be proud to be American—because no matter what Trump does or says, the majority disagrees, and that majority grows daily. This is the only country we have, and its future really is ours. Resist Trumpism, but reclaim your birthright as an American!

13

ACKNOWLEDGE, CHECK, AND USE YOUR PRIVILEGE

RECOMMENDED RESOURCES
Challenging White Supremacy Workshop
Citizenship and Social Justice Curriculum

WE'RE GOING TO be honest here, and perhaps a bit indelicate. But the topic requires it. In short: Ours is a broad-based movement. We don't have the conservative advantage of homogeneity—a movement dominated by older white men. We are ethnically, culturally, socially, and economically diverse. We have a broad spectrum of interests and points of view. That makes it difficult for liberals to arrive at a common message or consensus, but it's also our strength: our historic openness to diversity, combined with the steady influx of immigrants with new ideas and new energy, benefits liberalism the same way it has always benefited the United States as a nation.

The people who have historically dominated the leadership and direction of our party—mostly white and mostly male—can no longer hold on to and hide behind their privilege. The communities of color who make up an increasing percentage of our movement are no longer content to be relegated to the sidelines, brought out to play only when convenient (mostly around election time).

One big reason Bernie Sanders failed to seriously threaten Hillary Clinton in the race was his inability to connect with communities of color—the beating heart of the Democratic Party. His inner circle of advisers was exclusively white and male. His message about income inequality didn't speak to the immediate priorities of the Latino community, as it struggled to keep families intact in the face of immigration authorities; it was off-key in the African-American community. Having a good job didn't protect Sandra Bland from police brutality. And all the money in the world wouldn't (and didn't) protect women from that loser Donald Trump's unwanted sexual assaults (or those from Roger Ailes or Bill O'Reilly . . .).

That tone deafness manifested itself in various ways, such as minimizing the value of Southern primaries because those were red states in the general election. Well, those Southern Democratic primaries were dominated by black Democrats, and those were the one chance those voters of color had to have a real say in the presidential contest.

Thus, Bernie's dismissal of those Southern Democratic voters projected a message—regardless of intentions—that he didn't value communities of color. Yet Sanders partisans (and staff!) persisted in arguing the South didn't count, no matter how many times people tried to explain the damage their arguments were making. And in the end, that refusal to acknowledge issues of race cost Sanders dearly: 78 percent of black voters voted for Clinton, as did 65 percent of Latinos.

Sadly, the outcome only deepened resentment among many white progressives toward Democrats of color. A widely shared Facebook post by Gabriel Valdez read:

> *The Left Flank wonders why we vote differently from them while at the same time exhibiting the complete refusal to listen to us and what we need that makes us vote differently from them. Clinton won, our choice won, and when we asked for the alliance that people of color have been asked to give the choice of white voters for decades on end, the response was for white progressives to think it was beneath them. The thing we had been asked to do in order to hold a coalition together for generations was beneath white progressives. We've been asked to vote for our second, third, fourth choices so that we can hold the liberal alliance together. The minute we asked white progressives to do the same thing they've asked us to do, they were insulted. They wouldn't have it. They wouldn't lower themselves to help us the same way they've asked us to do. The gall of us to even ask.*

In other words, this is what these communities hear: 1) We white people know what's in your best interest better than you. 2) We'll identify the leaders, you just follow along in our "coalition." And 3) if you don't follow our wishes, we will abandon you.

"ESTABLISHMENT" IS A EUPHEMISM FOR . . .

Remember, this is not a battle between the "establishment" and "outsiders." That supposed "establishment" is one of the few places where women, blacks, and Latinos have any sort of governmental power (such as the Congressional Hispanic Caucus). And can anyone really argue that the communities of color who voted for Clinton are in any way representative of any truly powerful establishment?

But communities of color *will* support those who have been there for them in the past. Regardless of what you think about her politics, her history, or her husband, Hillary Clinton had a well-known, long, and solid history of standing by communities of color. The best Sanders' allies could do is dig up a picture of him marching in a civil rights rally in the 1960s. Clearly, Sanders is sensitive to racial justice issues, and his policy priorities are in the right place; no one has accused Sanders of being racist or overtly unfriendly to marginalized communities. But he has no history of *building relationships and political allegiances* with organized communities of color. Clinton has had those communities with her in her inner circle since the beginning of her political career; Sanders never bothered.

This is the crux of the problem: if you want someone with Sanders' politics to ever have a chance in a Democratic primary, and I suspect most of us reading this book do (as do the authors!), that person *has* to have deep credibility across the entire Democratic coalition. We promise you—there isn't a single person of color or woman pining for a white male savior. They are pining for a *partner* who understands their culture and language, willing to work in allegiance toward our movement's shared goals.

THERE ISN'T A SINGLE PERSON OF COLOR OR WOMAN PINING FOR A WHITE MALE SAVIOR. THEY ARE PINING FOR A *PARTNER*, WHO UNDERSTANDS THEIR CULTURE AND LANGUAGE, WILLING TO WORK IN ALLEGIANCE TOWARD OUR MOVEMENT'S SHARED GOALS.

We cannot emphasize this enough. The division between communities of color and white progressives is one of the biggest dangers to our long-term success. The divide must be bridged, and it will be bridged when we all:

1. **Work to *center* marginalized communities in all the political work you do**, not as foot soldiers, but in key leadership positions (and preferably, the *top* position). Support leaders of color and women by sharing their work on social media, donating to their efforts, and recruiting them to run for office.

2. **Defer to experience.** If you are a white progressive, understand that the personal fear you feel now toward Donald Trump is exactly how marginalized communities have felt . . . *since forever.* This may be new to you, but it's not to them. Respect their resilience because they are far more battle-tested than you are.

3. **LISTEN.** At countless political events, we've watched in wonder as white men interrupt and talk over women and people of color. Be mindful when you speak that you are not talking over anyone else. If some individuals aren't talking, pause and invite broader participation. Believe it or not, everyone already knows what white men think. And don't just "listen." *Listen.* Find areas of common ground or be challenged by new perspectives; resist the immediate urge to defend your position, and give air and

breath to what you've just heard. Ask yourself why you want so badly to counter or interrupt, and see what there is to learn about your response.

4. **Understand** that your threat level depends on your identity. You are less likely to be harassed by law enforcement if you're white. If arrested, you are more likely to receive lenient treatment if you're white. If you speak out, like on Twitter, you are less likely to endure a backlash of racist or sexist bile if you are a white male. Things are truly easier if you are white and male, so consider that the costs of activism aren't uniform across every demographic.

5. If you are a white male, **don't take this personally**. Once, after Markos had made some of these points on a *Daily Kos* blog post, a commenter sniffed, "I guess no one cares what white men think anymore!" Oh, we care. But when you are part of a real coalition, it means everyone's opinions matter as much as yours. That's not a bad thing, unless you are unwilling to surrender your preexisting privilege. Republicans are refusing to do so. We liberals are (supposedly) better than that.

6. **Know when to shut up.** You are not always the right person to be speaking on a matter or leading on an issue, so know when to shut up and sit all the way down. It's not about you. Stop making it about you.

People naturally build new networks based on their old networks, and those old networks are likely homogeneous and look exactly like them. But we cannot continue down our path, silo-ized by demographics. That means that the people who once wielded all the power have to surrender it in a power-sharing agreement. What emerges will be stronger, more cohesive, and more deeply, truly American than what we have today.

14

JOIN THE #BLACKLIVESMATTER MOVEMENT

RECOMMENDED RESOURCES

AskaWhitePerson.com
BlackLivesMatter.com
BlackLivesMatterSyllabus.com
CollectivePAC.org
ColorofChange.org
JoinCampaignZero.org
The Movement for Black Lives

BLACK LIVES MATTER was born in the summer of 2013, when Patrisse Cullors, Opal Tometi, and Alicia Garza started using the phrase as a Twitter hashtag. George Zimmerman had just been acquitted of murdering

Trayvon Martin for the crime of "walking with Skittles" through the gated community in which his father's fiancée lived.

The trio, like most in the African-American community, were distraught by the devaluation of black lives by police, district attorneys, judges, and juries—an issue long ignored by the American mainstream. The movement gained national prominence a year later after the police shooting death of an unarmed Michael Brown in Ferguson, Missouri. Rather than its being an isolated incident, the US Justice Department later found Ferguson had a "pattern and practice" of racial discrimination, "unlawfully" saddling its black residents with expensive tickets and fines—millions of dollars that the police then used for "revenue rather than public safety needs."

Since those tragedies, the pace of police violence and murder of black people only seems to have quickened.

- Twelve-year-old **Tamir Rice** was killed by police in Cleveland, on video, for playing with a toy pistol at a playground. The person who called 911 said the gun was "probably fake," but it didn't matter, because within *two seconds*, without any warning or demands to drop the gun, officer Timothy Loehmann shot to kill.
- **Rekia Boyd** was killed while partying in a park in Chicago. Police, as usual, claimed she had threatened the police with a gun, yet none was ever found. And as usual, the cop was acquitted.
- **Eric Garner** died in Staten Island, choked to death by police even as he wheezed out, "I can't breathe!"—again, on video. He was being arrested for illegally selling "loosies"—single cigarettes—in one of those "who gives a fuck" supposed crimes. Despite a New York Police Department ban on chokeholds, and despite the death being ruled a homicide by the medical examiner, a grand jury decided not to indict. Of course.

- **Sandra Bland,** on her way to a new job in Texas, was pulled over for a traffic violation in Waller County, supposedly for failing to signal a lane change. The arrestable crime? She refused to put out a cigarette on his command. Three days later, she ended up dead, hanging in her prison cell.

A thousand people are killed in the United States each year by police. Sixty percent of those people are either unarmed or involved in "quality of life" altercations, such as drug possession or mental crisis. Meanwhile, in 2011, police killed six in Germany, six in Australia, two in the United Kingdom, and zero in Japan.

Amid that carnage, there's a paradox: an American pop culture that celebrates and embraces black lives while doing nothing to stop the ongoing, state-sanctioned assault on black bodies. Black actress Amandla Stenberg asks, "What would America be like if we loved black people as much as we love black culture?"

When actor Jesse Williams accepted a BET Award for his role in *Grey's Anatomy* in 2016, he said:

> *We've been floating this country on credit for centuries, and we're done watching and waiting while this invention called whiteness uses and abuses us, burying black people out of sight and out of mind while extracting our culture, our dollars, our entertainment like oil—black gold!—ghettoizing and demeaning our creations and stealing them, gentrifying our genius and then trying us on like costumes before discarding our bodies like rinds of strange fruit. Just because we're magic doesn't mean we're not real.*

BAGGY JEANS AND RANK HYPOCRISY

The result: Suburban white teens wear baggy jeans, throw fake gang signs, and listen to Jay Z, while their conservative parents celebrate the relentless police assault on black communities and blather on about how "all lives matter" or "blue lives matter." Lily-white Fox News celebrities admonish black people for the parade of death, blaming them for not simply deferring to police—never mind that these same Fox personalities are the ones who endlessly warn of "tyrannical" government infringement on our constitutional freedoms.

**WHITE PEOPLE HAVE BEEN HEARD ALREADY.
NOW IS THE TIME TO FEATURE, HIGHLIGHT, AND
AMPLIFY BLACK VOICES.**

It gets worse. Police have no problem de-escalating confrontations with white suspects. It took law enforcement authorities *two years* to arrest Cliven Bundy after he led an armed standoff at his ranch over illegal cattle grazing, with snipers literally training their rifles on federal agents. Tamir Rice? He got the bullet after little more than two seconds.

So what can the broader, non-black Resistance movement do to enlist in the Black Lives Matter movement?

1. **Don't expect black people to educate you.** It's exhausting (and even harmful!) having to explain what should already be obvious. Educate yourself. Read *The New Jim Crow* and other materials listed in the Black Lives Matter Syllabus. Talk to other white people engaged in the struggle. In fact, one of the best roles for white allies is educating other whites. Make that your job.

2. **Check out the agenda at the Movement for Black Lives website.**

3. **Remind people that racism exists.** It's quite amazing how some people *still* think that President Barack Obama's presidency is proof that racism is on the decline. Quite the opposite, in fact. Trump's election is largely due to a massive racist backlash to the first African-American presidency. And that racism manifests itself in dramatic fashion in our justice system, from policing to incarceration to the courts—even into housing, who gets seated at restaurants, and who gets watched by security officers in retail outlets. So directly confront your racist uncle or high school friend on Facebook. Don't let their words fester unchallenged.

4. **Recognize the purpose of Trump's racist rhetoric.** Trump's bigotry, as University of Pennsylvania professor Salamishah Tillet notes, "[pulls] on our nation's history, in which these racial and sexual stereotypes of men and women have served a dual purpose: as a rhetorical shorthand to determine who and who does not deserve to be counted as an American citizen and as a longstanding justification for domestic terror against people of color." And that bigotry, not just against African-Americans, but against women, Latinos, Muslims, and other marginalized people, clearly struck a populist chord. It's pretty ugly out there, and we must confront that American reality.

5. **Black voices matter.** Be supportive, which means play a *supportive* role. Stay in the background unless specifically asked to come forward. White people have been heard already; this isn't your area of expertise—and it never will be. No matter how sincerely antiracist you are, you are still benefiting from centuries of oppression. So resist the urge to make it about you. Now is the time to feature, highlight, and amplify black voices. You are helping by being in the audience, by listening and learning.

6. **Watch your language.** As we discussed earlier, language matters. The desperate victims of Hurricane Katrina, abandoned by President Bush for days after one of the worst natural disasters in American history, were *scavenging* in New Orleans—not "looting." Every time you refer to a black victim or protester as a "thug," you are reinforcing dehumanizing language: it's the Right-wing media dog whistle for the N-word. No one referred to Cliven Bundy as a "thug," despite the fact that his snipers pointed their loaded weapons at law enforcement officials (a violation of basic gun safety protocol, not to mention state and federal law). They still didn't call them "thugs" when his armed adult children stormed and occupied a wildlife refuge in Oregon. Being white definitely has its privileges.

7. **Reject racist media tropes.** Every time a black person is murdered by police, people dig through that individual's background to declare that she or he "was no angel." Not being an "angel" isn't a capital crime in America—we're certainly not angels ourselves!—and a person doesn't have to be perfect to deserve their civil rights and the full protection of the law. In fact, this trope is so shopworn that it was trotted out against the elderly Asian doctor dragged out of an overbooked United flight in April 2017. Apparently, losing his medical license over a drug problem, a decade prior, was grounds to assault him for refusing to give up a seat he had paid for and had a right to use. Compare that to how the media excuses white actors of violence with words like "just a kid," "loner," "battling demons." Convicted rapist Brock Turner was described as a "Stanford student and star swimmer."

8. **Cede power.** We will never fulfill our true potential as a movement until we are fully integrated, one unified voice in common

resistance. That means that traditionally white groups (and even the new ones) must bring black leaders into decision-making positions of authority. If you are a leader in the movement, develop succession plans to distribute power in the future, and build a bench and pipeline to integrate and center black voices at all levels of an organization. The #BLM agenda should be part of every organization's work.

9. **Share success stories.** Help build up new black leadership by sharing the good work these leaders do. Too often, blacks only get covered in the white media in the context of crime, poverty, or tragedy. Move beyond the obvious artistic and athletic stories, and share business, civic, and political success stories.

10. **Show up.** Don't just support from afar. Be on the ground, ready to follow the leadership already there. White people always think they have better ideas about the protest, the action, the campaign, the messaging. *Always.* Black activists know how to organize and take action—they've been doing it as long as any other group in America! Follow their instructions. Maybe you'll learn something.

11. **Donate.** Every nonprofit advocacy org struggles to raise money. Donors give to people who look like them, so black groups struggle more than most. Wealth is concentrated within wealthy communities, and black people have far less access to it, by design. A lot of brilliant ideas never get acted upon due to lack of funding.

Lilla Watson, an Australian aboriginal activist, once distilled the collective thinking of Queensland aboriginal groups: "If you have come to help me, you are wasting your time. But if you have come because your liberation is bound up with mine, then let us work together."

That about sums it up: The black community is an integral component of the progressive coalition. We cannot be successful without it. The day the black community no longer has to worry about being shot by police, or being crushed by an unfair justice system, that's the day it can refocus on broader issues like income inequality and climate change. Our destinies are intertwined. It is imperative we stand in unwavering solidarity in the struggle for justice and equality.

15

HELP REFUGEES AND OTHER IMMIGRANTS IN YOUR COMMUNITY

RECOMMENDED RESOURCES

AmericanImmigrationCouncil.org

AmericasVoice.org

BorderAngels.org

Council on American-Islamic Relations

Church World Service

Hi.org

InformedImmigrant.com

LatinoVictory.us

National Immigration Law Center

OneAmericaRegistry.org

Presente.org

Soundvision.com

WeAreHeretoStay.org

WelcomingAmerica.org

THE UNITED STATES is a nation of immigrants, founded by religious refugees fleeing persecution in Europe. Since those early days of European settlement, our population has been steadily fed by wave after wave of immigrants, many of whom came for new opportunities—and many of whom came to escape their own persecution. Regardless of motivation, each and every immigrant has helped weave our uniquely American, multicultural tapestry.

Despite being the core of who we are as a people, that same rich diversity is viewed by the Republican base as an existential threat. How can one remain wedded to an idyllic past when people who look, act, speak, and eat differently keep moving in? So rather than try to ideologically appeal to these newcomers, the message has been curt and simple: stay out.

As one piece on Breitbart put it: "The alt-right believe that some degree of separation between peoples is necessary for a culture to be preserved." Donald Trump took those words literally; he launched his campaign promising a dividing wall, paid for by Mexico, and built off that racist foundation by demanding a Muslim ban. Whether he manages to achieve either is irrelevant; he's already created a culture of terror in immigrant communities and unleashed the immigration authorities, who are rounding up undocumented immigrants by the thousands—even those without a criminal record.

It is thus our responsibility to protect immigrant communities and help keep families together, whether they have the proper documentation or not. It is our duty to help refugee families, still hurting from the trauma of war and conflict, build a new home in a strange land. And it's not just a moral imperative; we need to be true allies to each other if we're to build a unified movement. Just as it's important to support Black Lives Matter, it is important to be there for Latino, Asian, Muslim, and other immigrant communities.

So what can people do to help?

1. **Be a friend** to a refugee. When people arrive, they have no clue how to navigate unfamiliar terrain in a foreign language. They need help figuring out things like public transit, finding a place of worship, getting a library card, and enrolling their children in school.

2. **Offer space** in your home for newly arrived refugees.

3. **Donate** to organizations supporting immigrants and refugees, or host a fundraiser on their behalf.

4. **Donate your skills.** When the first travel ban was implemented, lawyers flooded airports, setting up temporary offices in lounges and working together—pro bono—to assist those trapped by the order. Be alert to opportunities to wield your skills, connections, and knowledge in assistance.

5. **Call your elected officials.** We already talked about how much this works. Keep doing it when immigration-related issues come up for votes.

6. **Combat xenophobia on social media.** Don't let Twitter trolls or your racist aunt on Facebook get away with bigotry. Push back, wherever intolerance arises.

7. **Make immigrants in your community feel welcome.** Post signs at home or at your business welcoming immigrants. Send a message that you are not part of Trump's racist America.

8. **Urge your community to become a Sanctuary City.** Donald Trump hates sanctuary cities—municipalities that refuse to assist federal immigration authorities in their quest to break families apart. Lobby your municipal elected officials to be welcoming to all.

9. **Lobby your church to join the "holy resistance."** The Church

World Service, a cooperative ministry of thirty-seven Christian denominations, saw its number of sanctuary congregations double to eight hundred after the election. "Congregations have been knocking down our doors," said Reverend Noel Andersen of the Church World Service. "We expect more because of the outcry from our congregations that we've heard." Work to get your church, synagogue, or mosque to welcome and support immigrants.

10. **Economically support immigrants.** Shop at their businesses, use their services, hire them at work.

11. **Sabotage government xenophobia.** When the Trump regime launched their "VOICE hotline" to report immigration-related crime, it was bombarded by people reporting crime by space aliens. (The number is 1-855-48-VOICE, if you want to give it a shot now!) If Trump ever gets his Muslim registry off the ground, we'll sabotage that too. If you see ICE agents preparing for a raid, call your contacts in immigration communities to sound the alarm.

Not only is fighting for immigrant and refugee rights in sync with American values and common human decency, it's also good politics. Collectively, communities of color will be the American majority by 2039, and Latinos will surpass whites to be the largest racial/ethnic group around 2043 according to the Pew Research Center and U.S. census data. While smaller in absolute numbers, Asians are the fastest growing ethnic group in the country. African and Muslim immigrant communities are growing rapidly in places like Minnesota and Michigan—key presidential battlegrounds. If Republicans want to cede the future of America to progressives, that's their prerogative. It is our responsibility and honor—as liberals, as Americans, *and* as decent human beings—to be there for those immigrant communities.

16

FIGHT RAPE CULTURE AND SEXUAL HARASSMENT

RECOMMENDED RESOURCES

ALongWalkHome.org
GenerationFive.org
Incite-National.org
LoveArmy.org
MenStoppingViolence.org
NotheRapeDocumentary.org

IT WAS LATE in the campaign cycle, early October 2016, when the bombshell tape emerged: a recording of popular-vote loser Donald Trump talking with *Access Hollywood* host Billy Bush about the women he sexually assaulted. "I'm automatically attracted to beautiful [women]—I just start kissing them," he said. "It's like a magnet. Just kiss. I don't even wait. And when you're a star they let you do it. You can do anything. . . . Grab them by the pussy. You can do anything." He refused to apologize for the words, dismissing them as "locker room banter," as if the setting (which wasn't a locker room anyway) did anything to lessen the impact (and import) of his words.

Feminist Jessica Valenti has written, "Rape is a standard result of a culture mired in misogyny, but for whatever reason—denial, self-preservation, sexism—Americans bend over backwards to make excuses for male violence." And nowhere was that more clear than at the ballot box last year, where every single vote Trump got was a national disgrace, including the 41 percent of women who voted for him. Despite the fact that he outright admitted to being a sexual predator, too many in America validated his behavior with their vote anyway. People have spent decades trying to impress on men that "no means no" (much better formulated, these days, as "yes means yes"), only to have Trump single-handedly undermine women's rights and legitimize sexual predation, assault, harassment, and discrimination. This isn't a shame that will wash away easily, if ever.

But the macho aggressiveness displayed by Trump and further embodied in the Republican Party isn't about lust or sexual self-control; it's a tool deployed to exert power, control, and oppression. "It is part of the larger epidemic of violence against women that preserves our system and social practice of male dominance and gender inequity," explains Salamishah Tillet.

Among too many men, women are still expected to stay in their place—preferably in the kitchen. And that isn't an outdated belief, the province of just the elderly. University of Michigan's long-running Monitoring the Future survey of the attitudes of millennials found this year that support among high school seniors for egalitarian families has fallen, with those wanting women to stay home with the children rising to 58 percent in 2014, compared to 42 percent in 1994. In 1994, 29 percent of male high school seniors thought "the husband should make all the important decisions in the family." By 2014, that figure had risen to 37 percent.

GIRL, INTERRUPTED

Perhaps boys are conditioned to believe this because of what they see in the world around them. In a George Washington University study, twenty women and twenty men were put in pairs and asked to talk for three minutes. Their conversations were then recorded and transcribed. The number of interruptions was then counted. As it turns out, women interrupted men just once per conversation, while the men interrupted women 2.8 times. Men interrupted their male counterparts twice per conversation; females interrupted other women 2.6 times. Men aren't used to being interrupted. Women seem to do nothing *but* get interrupted.

Another 1998 meta-study of forty-three different studies at the University of California–Santa Cruz found that men were more likely to interrupt to take control of a conversation (as opposed to encourage or reinforce a point a woman was making); that instinct was elevated in group settings. Studies have also found that men dominate professional meetings, in classrooms, and even in hospitals, where men were more likely to interrupt female doctors than male ones. And while women make up 62 percent of all Twitter users, men are twice as likely to be retweeted as women.

Republicans certainly reinforce those ugly sociological trends. In the US Senate in early 2017, Republican Senate majority leader

Mitch McConnell and his all-male leadership team (of course) censured Massachusetts Democrat Elizabeth Warren for reading a letter of opposition to then–attorney general nominee Jeff Sessions written by Coretta Scott King, Martin Luther King's widow. McConnell didn't censure Texas Republican Sen. Ted Cruz when he called McConnell a liar on the Senate floor, on more than one occasion. He didn't censor Arkansas Republican senator Tom Cotton when he referred to Democratic Senate minority leader Harry Reid's "cancerous leadership." When it comes to Trump and McConnell and the rest of the GOP, they echo that survey of millennial men: "shut up, women, let *us* make the important decisions."

The Resistance must fight to limit the damage Trump and his party are doing to our culture. So what can we do? Borrowing from Valenti's anthology *Yes Means Yes*, and other sources:

1. **For heaven's sake, don't blame the victim!** Whenever an instance of rape makes the news, people immediately question the victim's attire, attitude, or sobriety. People will utter inanities like "Boys will be boys!" or "slutshame" the victim to excuse violent masculinity. "Here's a tip: the right question is not, 'What was she doing/wearing/saying when she was raped?'" Valenti writes. "The right question is, 'What made him think this is acceptable?'"

2. **Reimagine masculinity.** It's easy to see, watching the reaction to loser Trump dropping that massive MOAB bomb on Afghanistan, how violence is treated as a masculine trait. Trump was "tough" for asking someone else to order someone else to fly a plane, over a nation with no air defenses, to drop a bomb that killed untold numbers of people, irrespective of their innocence. Manly! Except there's no reason that masculinity and violence must be intertwined. Stop equating the two.

3. **Forget "no means no." Look for YES.** After an assault, people shouldn't be wondering whether the victim is emphatic or clear in saying no. Consider Trump, assaulting women in such a way that they don't even have the *opportunity* to say no. If the standard for consensual sex is an *enthusiastic yes,* it eliminates any possible ambiguity.

4. **Fight negative portraits of women in media.** Whether it's the news, an ad campaign, or a movie, oppose the disrespectful or derogatory portrayal of women, and support the treatment of women as equal humans, with full acknowledgment of their agency over their bodies.

5. **Be intersectional.** Issues of violence and masculinity have an impact beyond rape culture: they deeply affect LGBTQ people. Gay, transgendered, and gender-nonconforming people suffer violence at rates disproportionate to their population. Meanwhile, people of different races and incomes do not have the same level of access to the justice system as more privileged groups. We must protect the most marginalized groups.

6. **Enforce community standards—online and off.** Report abuse on social media sites like Twitter. Don't let overt sexism stand unchallenged in your environment, whether at work, at home, or in the virtual world.

7. **Don't interrupt women and man-splain.** Don't be Kanye rushing the stage, taking the microphone away from Taylor Swift. Don't interrupt women, don't dismiss what they say, don't diminish their words or work. If you are in a mixed group, and the men are dominating the discussion, invite women to share their thoughts. If a man steps over a woman in your presence, make it clear that's not okay and urge the woman to finish her thoughts.

8. **Encourage young girls to trust their instincts—and believe them.** Women are taught to always second-guess themselves and are constantly gaslighted (manipulated into questioning their own sanity) about their own experiences.

9. **Teach young boys to respect women.** Make sure boys know that misogyny is not allowed, and that people like Trump who practice it are not good people. Be forceful and direct, and as a father, caregiver, friend, or acquaintance, model good, respectful behavior.

This is not always easy stuff to do. Many of us have to unlearn deeply ingrained misogynistic behaviors. But being mindful of our shortcomings is the first step; greater awareness will help build a movement in which all of us respect each other. Just as is the case with people of color and immigrant communities, there is no progressive movement without women. We are only as strong externally as we are united internally.

That means we must treat women as full equal partners—in our everyday lives and in our political efforts.

PROTECT REAL RELIGIOUS LIBERTIES

RECOMMENDED RESOURCES

BreachRepairers.org
Council on American-Islamic Relations
Matthew25Pledge.com
Sojo.net

FOR DECADES, CONSERVATIVES have proclaimed themselves champions of "religious liberty." In theory, this should be uncontroversial: "religious liberty" should mean that whatever your views on religion—whether you're practicing or nonpracticing—you should be free to practice (or not practice) those views as you see fit, provided, of course, you obey all the other laws we live by.

That's the beauty of a secular state like America: it has room for people of all faiths and makes no special treatment for any.

In reality, conservatives don't actually believe in religious liberty: they see secular governance as a threat to their religious values, and they're working to make all Americans subservient to the theocratic, radical Christianist wing of their party. Their approach has more in common with the ayatollahs in Iran and the Taliban in Afghanistan than with our nation's Jeffersonian founding principles. Because if you're not a white Christian, conservatives aim to use the power of government to curtail your right to worship, or *not* to worship, as you see fit.

Nothing makes clearer this conservative bastardization of "religious freedom" than a letter sent by one hundred religious-right leaders asking Donald Trump to allow adoption providers to discriminate against same-sex households, send federal dollars to schools and businesses that discriminate on the basis of sexual orientation, permit military chaplains to preach discrimination from their pulpits, and bless religious schools' efforts to prohibit their students from using contraception.

"We urge you to take action to ensure their freedom to believe and live out those beliefs is protected from government punishment," the letter concluded. "We, in the conservative movement, stand ready to assist you in your efforts to protect and uphold the freedom of religion in America."

The existence of these organizations isn't being threatened; their individual members are free to practice their religion how they see fit. But their *claimed right to discriminate*—and use the power of government to back their discrimination—is not an actual right, not in the United States, anyway. They can practice whatever beliefs they like in their homes and in their places of worship, but the US government does not permit any form of religious bigotry in any public accommodation—be it a business, a school, or a government facility.

In short, religious discrimination violates the very core of what makes America *America*.

"SEE YOU IN COURT," SAID TRUMP, TO THE COURTS

Of course, neither the plain language of the law nor multiple federal court rulings against him has stopped Trump from trying to ban Muslims from entering the country. Couched in the language of "security," the ban attempts were a thinly veiled effort to manufacture an indelible link between Islam and terrorism—to convince reactionary white Americans that the only way they can be safe is to stem the inflow of Muslims in the country. It didn't matter that there is no history of refugee-fueled terrorism in this country. It was racist, religious fear-mongering, straight out of the pages of Breitbart, and a direct assault on true religious liberties.

The absurdity of the religious debate came into sharp focus in a February 2017 Pew poll on the travel ban. The survey found that 38 percent of Americans approved of the ban, while 59 percent of patriotic Americans opposed it. But the strongest support for the ban—by far—came from white evangelical Protestants (in effect, the religious Right), with *76 percent* approving. Among Catholics, 62 percent *opposed*, and among religiously unaffiliated respondents, it was the inverse of the religious bigots, with 74 percent opposing. Among racial groups, 49 percent of whites approved of the ban, compared to just 17 percent of Latinos and 11 percent of blacks.

Got that? The same people braying about "religious freedoms" are first in line to cleanse America of any non-Christians! Republicans want you to do as they *say*, not as they *do*.

TARGETING (NON-CHRISTIAN) DESCENDANTS OF ABRAHAM

In Trump's America, it's not just Muslims under fire. As has been the case for millennia when demagogues take control, the Jewish faith is also under assault. In just one week in March 2017, three Jewish cemeteries were vandalized, in Saint Louis, Philadelphia, and New York. In Philadelphia, nearly one hundred tombstones were knocked over. Two neighboring Christian cemeteries remained untouched. (Proving themselves patriots, the Muslim community rallied in support, raising over $130,000 to pay for repairs and sending volunteers to assist with the cleanup.)

There have been dozens of similar incidents. The number of hate crimes in New York City was up an astonishing 94 percent at the beginning of 2017; nationally, the number of anti-Jewish hate incidents increased 21 percent in 2014, and 27 percent in 2015, according to the Anti-Defamation League. When the 2016 numbers are tallied, they will almost assuredly show yet another increase. And already, 2017 is set to crush those numbers—anti-Semitic incidents increased a whopping 86 percent in the first three months of 2017, compared to the same period in 2016. "We're definitely seeing an uptick in reporting—and that's actually why it takes longer to go through this data and verify everything," said Oren Segal, director of the ADL's Center on Extremism. "It was happening before Election Day, but definitely since Election Day, we've seen an uptick. We've never seen anything like this before."

Of course, it's not surprising that a White House infested by "white nationalists" like Steve Bannon and neo-Nazis like Sebastian Gorka (who is linked to the far-right Hungarian group Vitézi Rend, which has been labeled by the US State Department as "under the direction of the Nazi Government of Germany" during World War II, according to Forward.com) is adding fuel to the fire. During a question from Jewish reporter in mid-February 2017 about Trump's lack of public statements about the rise of anti-Semitic acts, Trump interrupted to bark, "It's not a fair question. Sit down." He wrapped up by proclaiming, "I'm the least anti-Semitic person you've seen in your entire life," although no one at that news conference had accused him of being anti-Semitic.

Still, if Trump is the least anti-Semitic person anyone has seen, he has a funny way of showing it. In January 2017, his staff omitted any reference to Jews in the White House's statement on Holocaust Remembrance Day. Then in April, during Passover, White House spokesman Sean Spicer claimed that the Nazis weren't as bad as Syrian dictator Bashar al-Assad because they "never used chemical weapons against their own people." When reminded of the mass murder of six million Jews—many by poison gas—Spicer stammered out nonsense about "Holocaust centers," which was just weird. And just as damning was the fact that Spicer didn't see German Jews as being Hitler's "own people." Apparently, to him, just like his bosses, they were something *other*.

GET UP, STAND UP

The rise in anti-Semitism and anti-Islamic bigotry is being fueled, if not encouraged, by the White House, with their election victory validating the message of their ugly racist campaign. Thus, it is our job as progressives to fight for the right of people to worship how they see fit, regardless of the deity they pray (or don't pray) to. Protesting the Muslim ban sent a stronger message to the world about where America *really* stands on religious freedom than any words from Trump, or bigoted letters from conservative faith leaders, or even polls showing that Americans are disgusted with Trump's ban.

So how do we truly protect religious liberty? Protesters standing against the Muslim ban at Detroit Metropolitan Airport gave us a huge clue: "Someone came around at 6 p.m. and said, "Hey look, it's time for their prayer, so we're going to make a circle around them so they can do that with love and protection," protester Jeena Patel recounted to local media outlet MLive. "People put down their signs, knowing that the people who would be praying would have to kneel—so they wouldn't have to do it on the wet concrete. Everyone just quieted down. It was a really moving moment."

The circle provided a safe space for the two dozen Muslims to practice their faith, respectfully, as Americans. We owe it to people of all faiths and creeds to ensure they too feel safe—in their places of worship, in public parks and plazas, in shops and businesses. The Resistance must stand against the establishment of any single state-sanctioned religion, so that all religions can flourish.

18

FIGHT BULLYING IN SCHOOLS

RECOMMENDED RESOURCES

StopBullying.gov
Tyler Clementi Foundation

IT WAS ONE of those surreal moments, an alternate universe where Melania Trump could be considered a first lady in the tradition of Lady Bird Johnson, Eleanor Roosevelt, or Hillary Clinton: a thoughtful, powerful woman, in the White House, with a cause. Just days before the presidential election—an election that depended substantially on online bullying by right-wing copycats of her weak bully of a husband—Melania dared to proclaim at a Pennsylvania campaign appearance shortly before the election:

Our culture has gotten too mean and too violent. It is never okay when a 12-year-old girl or boy is mocked, bullied or attacked. It is terrible when that happens on the playground and it is unacceptable when it's done by someone with no name hiding on the Internet.

The irony was apparently lost on both Republicans and the "centrist" media; of course, there's no bigger bully in American political history than popular-vote loser Donald Trump, who has always used his position of privilege and wealth (and now political power) to verbally belittle his opponents. Whether mocking a disabled reporter in public, or calling people who didn't vote for him "losers," or bragging about sexually assaulting women, or demonizing Latinos and Muslims and anyone who opposes him, or belittling a Jewish reporter on Holocaust Remembrance Day—no insult is too low for Donald Trump.

"THE TRUMP CAMPAIGN . . . HAS NOT JUST CREATED MORE RACIAL RESENTMENT, BUT IT'S ALSO GIVEN OXYGEN TO THE EMBERS OF RESENTMENT AND FANNED THOSE FLAMES."

Trump has a bully pulpit in both the literal and metaphorical sense, and he seems to rather enjoy using it.

So for the next four years, we'll have to guard against the man who serves as the nation's chief role model—and make sure our kids know the only role Trump is suited for is filling a spot in a prison cell. His behavior should get him shunned and ostracized and his criminal acts should get him convictions—not a reward as leader of the free world.

As comedian Aziz Ansari said on *Saturday Night Live*:

I'm talking about this tiny slice of people that have gotten way too fired up about the Trump thing for the wrong reasons. I'm talking about these people that, as soon as Trump won, they're, like, "We don't have to pretend like we're not racist anymore! We don't have to pretend anymore! We can be racist again! Whoo!" Whoa, whoa, whoa! No, no! If you're one of these people, please go back to pretending.

SAVING THE KIDS—AND OUR FUTURE—FROM TRUMPISM

Hopefully, it's not too late. After the election, the Southern Poverty Law Center conducted a survey of ten thousand educators, and the results were distressing. "Ninety percent of educators report that the school climate has been negatively affected, and most of them believe it will have a long-lasting impact," read the report titled "The Trump Effect: The Impact of the 2016 Presidential Election on Our Nation's Schools." The report continues:

> *A full 80 percent describe heightened anxiety and concern on the part of students worried about the impact of the election on themselves and their families. . . . The behavior is directed against immigrants, Muslims, girls, LGBT students, kids with disabilities and anyone who was on the "wrong" side of the election. It ranges from frightening displays of white power to remarks that are passed off as "jokes."*

Another 2016 survey of 50,000 thirteen-to-eighteen-year-olds by the Human Rights Campaign found that 70 percent of respondents had witnessed bullying, hate messages, or harassment since the start of the last election season. Seventy percent of those incidents were race-motivated, 63 percent were based on sexual orientation, 59 percent were based on immigration status, and 55 percent were related to sex and gender. Trump's success "has given permission and legitimated what was previously considered illegitimate," Robert Faris, a sociology professor at the University of California–Davis told *Mother Jones* magazine. "The Trump campaign, in my view, has not just created more racial resentment, but it's also given oxygen to the embers of resentment and fanned those flames."

FOMENTING RACIAL RESENTMENT—IN OUR SCHOOLS

The bullying has become so brazen, in fact, that in some places, students have openly celebrated and promoted their bigotry. In North Texas, students attending predominantly white Archer City High School chanted, "Build that wall!" at a volleyball match. The opposing school, located in West Texas, near the Mexican border, was predominantly Latino. One of the Latino students posted about the event on Facebook, "No doubt in my mind that this sentiment has always existed with groups of people but to display it so openly is so not correct!"

Similar ugliness arose in a high school basketball game in New Jersey, between predominantly white Jefferson Township High School and Dover High School, which is 80 percent black and Latino. "When one of our African-American students attempted to make foul shots, a small group of the home team fans chanted 'Ashy knees,'" Dover's athletic director wrote in a complaint to their governing athletic organization. "When the Dover students were warming up, chants of 'Build the wall' resounded from another small, yet vocal group of fans. A variety of racial slurs were also expressed during the game."

Much of the burden for fighting this bullying falls on educators. Teachers and administrators on the front lines of this epidemic must be trained to handle these matters. But we can certainly press school boards to have effective school bullying strategies, as well as advocate for increased funding for those efforts.

We must use every opportunity to impress upon our children that what Trump says, what he does, and the actions of his racist administration are not okay (I'm looking at you, Jeff Sessions—but also you, Steve Bannon and Gorka and Stephen Miller and . . .). The behavior they see modeled by this White House is the behavior of monsters and bullies, not responsible adult citizens.

We should also make sure our kids feel comfortable speaking up when they are the target of such bullying or when they witness someone else being targeted; silence is complicity. And since not all bullying is political, we must reinforce our own liberal values of helping others, displaying compassion and tolerance, and providing an alternative positive role model for the leaders of tomorrow.

19

CREATE ART FOR THE RESISTANCE

RECOMMENDED RESOURCES

AmericansfortheArts.org
BadandNasty.com
CreativesinAction.net
StealThisPrint.com

THE USE OF art for political ends is as old as art and politics themselves. In the United States, Benjamin Franklin drew the famous cartoon of the divided snake, with the caption "Join, or Die," as a warning to the colonies that they could only survive united as one. Paul Revere's copper engraving of the Boston Massacre in 1770, depicting British forces mowing down unarmed blood-splattered civilians, helped rally anti-British sentiment.

Whether it's Rosie the Riveter in World War II or the iconic Shepard Fairey "Change" Obama poster, art has the power to motivate, to move, to inspire, and to engage. And in this digital era, the idea of political art has evolved beyond physical media, to the use of "memes" on social media and other online outlets. You can even see this in action with the American Right. While conservatives generally lack artistic talent—creative types tend not to be the mouth-breathing conformists who populate the GOP—they have appropriated the symbols of American patriotism for themselves, from the flag to culture icons like the bald eagle. No need to be creative when you can just take your nation's national symbols for yourself.

Political movements thrive on the bandwagon effect. The more people around you are engaged politically, the more engaged you will become. People want to be *part* of something, rather than an island unto themselves. So anything that reinforces a common and *popular* cause is beneficial to the effort. Conservatives buy books by authors like Ann Coulter knowing they will never read a damn page. Rather, they want to see those authors at the top of the bestseller lists, validating their ideology. Trump insists on having physical rallies to create that sense of shared purpose and popularity. Polls showing his unpopularity are abstract numbers on a page; in the minds of participants, a crowd of thousands is infinitely more *real*.

SPEAK SOFTLY, AND CARRY A BIG CAN OF SPRAY PAINT

Whether we choose to admit it or not, the imagery we surround ourselves with has a deep and lasting impact on our behavior and beliefs, so it's important to infuse our quotidian lives with subtle, incisive, and biting political commentary that speaks to people—without necessarily using words.

We need to reinforce the anti-Republican message everywhere people look, everywhere they visit, with every conversation they have. Art is perfectly suited for this kind of work. Political graffiti can reinforce anti-Trump sentiment, as can having a Facebook feed stocked with anti-Trump memes. (Conservatives were very good at reinforcing their bubble online with anti-Clinton and anti-Obama filth.)

We're already seeing artists engage fully in the Resistance. Comic artists have gleefully reimagined the cover of the first Captain America comic book, which depicts a muscle-bound superhero punching Hitler in the face; in the new versions, Hitler is replaced by Donald Trump, Steve Bannon, and other top Republicans. In another popular version, Captain America is replaced by Ms. Marvel, who in the current Marvel universe is a teenage Muslim Pakistani. (Once again, art is on the bleeding edge of cultural change.)

Other comic-book-related memes include images with Superman captioned "Refugee" (as he arrived from a destroyed planet Krypton) and Wonder Woman captioned "Immigrant" (from the island paradise Themyscira). Disney artist Nikkolas Smith reimagined Trump as *The Incredibles* villain Syndrome.

THE SAN FRANCISCO MURAL CULTIVATING RESISTANCE FEATURES A TINY-HANDED TRUMP SURROUNDED BY TWITTER BIRDS LABELED "LIES," "MISOGYNY," "ISLAMOPHOBIA," AND "XENOPHOBIA."

Neighborhood street artists are also getting in on the action, with amazing works popping up all over the country:

- In San Francisco's Mission District, the San Francisco Poster Syndicate has posted a brilliant mural titled *Cultivating Resistance*. It features a tiny-handed Trump surrounded by Twitter birds labeled "lies," "misogyny," "Islamophobia," and "xenophobia." All around are symbols of the decay of American democracy—a classical-looking building crumbling, pipelines spewing oil, lines of riot police, Steve Bannon wearing the white robes of the KKK and holding a judge's gavel, bulldozers, and flames. At the bottom, the tree of liberty is being watered by a black man and a Native American man, while a woman in Muslim garb holds hands with a Latina-looking woman with a baby.

- An anti-Trump billboard in Phoenix drapes Trump's ugly mug with mushroom clouds and two swastika-style dollar signs. On the backside, five multicolored hands spell out, in American sign language, "Unity," as the same word is emblazoned above. "Billboards are perfect because you don't have to go to a gallery to see it," said its creator, Karen Fiorito, who received death threats for the work. "You're creating a dialogue with the public. You're reaching people you'd never reach with your artwork."

- In New York, street artist Hanksy painted Trump as a pile of shit. Los Angeles artist Illma Gore painted a portrait of Trump nude, with a, shall we say, *artistic interpretation* of the source of Trump's likely feelings of inadequacy. Of course, Trump's legal team threatened to sue.

- Shepard Fairey is also once again creating iconic art. His trio prints of women—one African-American, one Latina, and one a Muslim wearing an American flag-print hijab—are now commonly seen at protests, and hanging in the homes and storefronts of Resistance fighters.

THE PINK PUSSYHATS GRAB TRUMP BY THE BALLS

Of course, there are few pieces of Trump protest art more ubiquitous than the famous pink pussyhats that adorned the heads of tens of thousands of protesters. The hats were made, by hand, by thousands of individuals.

"I think having that visual creates an impetus for people to really get involved," said Pussyhat Project cocreator Jayna Zweiman. "For people who are knitters and not marchers, it's a way of representing themselves. To physically make something is really special in this day and age where a lot of stuff is very virtual. [The knitters] have the opportunity to send a note to a marcher, so they connect with someone directly if they want to. It's great for both introverts and extroverts." Knitting stores around the country ran out of pink yarn as over a hundred thousand of these hats were made for the Women's March.

For the artists and performers among us, Bad and Nasty, a collective of artists "committed to channeling art and anger into activism, into action," has a guide to organizing an anti-Trump show. If you're so inclined, you can take it upon yourself to network with local artists to identify opportunities for creative activism.

> **KNITTING STORES AROUND THE COUNTRY RAN OUT OF PINK YARN AS OVER A HUNDRED THOUSAND PINK PUSSYHATS WERE MADE FOR THE WOMEN'S MARCH.**

If you're an artist, or have creative talents you want to put to use for the Resistance, attend other meetings, like Indivisible, and see how you can contribute to their mission. For example, in Portland, Maine, a local group called Get Ready Weekly gathers volunteers to design and paint signs for protests and to create politically themed memes to distribute online.

For everyone else, if you see a great piece of political art, snap a picture and post it to social media. Provide political artists with validation—both verbal and the cash kind. Go to StealThisPrint.com and download and print political posters to post around town.

The more people see and hear signs of the Resistance, the more ingrained the idea of resisting will become. Nurture that idea with fun, creative, and memorable art, and watch it grow.

20

TAKE TIME OFF AND RECOVER

ADMIT IT: THIS Donald Trump thing has knocked you completely off-kilter. Sure, it's exciting to work in solidarity with so many amazing people in the Resistance, but it's also exhausting to endure the relentless stream of setbacks and bad news. Many of the norms of civic behavior and institutions we care about are being destroyed. *People* we care about are being hurt; some will actually die. If you are a person of color, Trump's presidency is an existential threat. If you are a white liberal, well, now you know how everyone else has felt since forever. We have every reason to be anxious!

Many of us in the Resistance are glued to the news, checking Twitter obsessively to hear about the latest Trump indignities. We take action, and when we run out of actions, we putz around nervously, afraid we aren't doing *enough*. We work during the day; then we work at night and on weekends. For the resistance. There is no break. How could we take time off when so much damage is being done to our country?

But here's the thing—this obsession is messing up your life. We all need to be alert, emotionally available, and fresh at various times over the next four years, to block bad legislation, to block bad government actions, to protect our allies. If you are burning political energy at 110 percent right now, there's no way you'll be able to sustain the pace—and you *will* burn out. We've seen it too often (in fact, this same advice extends to many leaders in the progressive movement).

Your anxiety doesn't just impede your effectiveness in the Resistance; it impacts everyone around you—your spouse, your children, your friends and colleagues, anyone you have more than a passing relationship with.

This isn't the same thing as *pacing* yourself, which implies a steady level of Resistance activity. An active Resistance will be full of peaks and valleys; it's *essential* that you use the valleys to recover—just like a cyclist recovers on the flats and downhills, or elite athletes plan "recovery days" between intense training sessions, you've *got* to rest for the steep climbs ahead. So here's what you need to do:

- **Unplug from the news.** Trust me, Trump will do something despicable today and tomorrow and the day after. And when you return from your time off, catching up is easy to do. So unplug for a day or a weekend or a week.

- **Reconnect with those who give you purpose.** There's a reason all of us are fighting in this Resistance. It could be for our children and their future, or for our friends, or for our families or communities. Spending time with those people will remind you why you fight, and give you a renewed energy and sense of purpose when you reengage.

- **Practice self-care.** Don't let the loser asshole in the White House destroy your life. Eat healthy, get plenty of sleep, exercise, do yoga, meditate, read some fiction. Go to the spa, binge-watch a new show on Netflix, take in a ball game, play Xbox—whatever it is that helps you relax. The better your physical and mental health, the sharper your Resistance work will be. The healthier your body, the more stamina and longevity you'll have. We need you around for the long haul.

- **Leave your house.** A sports event, concert, or performance can help you forget how Trump wants nuclear Armageddon with North Korea. Go for a hike, or to a park or beach and soak up energy from the great outdoors.

- **Stop feeling guilty!** Taking time off isn't an indulgence. It's biologically necessary for health and sanity. Allowing yourself time to recover will make you a better Resistance fighter.

The most important person in the world is you, followed closely by your loved ones. Take care of both, and the former will give you strength and endurance, while the latter will give you purpose. We're in this for the long haul. Sorry to say, but the fight against conservatism will outlast Trump's presidential term. So taking time off won't damage the Resistance effort. To the contrary, it will help ensure its long-term success.

MINIMIZE DAMAGE, POLICY

21

LEAK LIKE A SIEVE

RECOMMENDED RESOURCES

AmericanBridgePAC.org
CitizensforEthics.org
DemocraticCoalition.org/leaks
Freedom.press
WhistleBlowers.org

DONALD TRUMP IS running one of the most secretive administrations in American history. Breaking from established White House policy, his regime will no longer publish visitor logs, ensuring that taxpayers have zero insight into who is meeting with Trump and his lieutenants in the White House—which is owned by taxpayers. For a guy who ran on "draining the swamp," he's actually making it quite cozy and comfortable for DC's alligators.

And yet, paradoxically, this may be the *leakiest* White House ever.

Trump's ignorant, hands-off approach to both policy *and* staff management has created a world in which competing factions work to undermine each other for personal gain, unconcerned about how stupid they make their boss look. Meanwhile, the regime's ham-fisted attack on the federal bureaucracy has led to surreptitious efforts to undermine Trump's agenda from the inside.

When Trump took office, he ordered employees at agencies like the Environmental Protection Agency, the Department of the Interior, and Health and Human Services to delete website pages dealing with things such as science and facts and data used by researchers to advance our understanding of the world. Not keen to see their life's work decimated, agency employees responded with resistance: they created nearly fifty "alt" agency Twitter accounts, with rogue federal employees using social media outlets to circumvent Trump's ideologically based gag orders.

Meanwhile, the same intelligence agencies that Trump has repeatedly attacked as incompetent carefully leaked details about their investigation into Trump's Russia ties.

It is clear these leaks severely undermine and anger Trump, who has made a habit of railing against the leakers. In January 2017, before taking office, he reacted to intelligence leaks about the Russian investigation by tweeting, "Intelligence agencies should never have allowed this fake news to 'leak' into the public. One last shot at me. Are we living in Nazi Germany?" In mid-February 2017 he followed up with, "The real story here is why are there so many illegal leaks coming out of Washington? Will these leaks be happening as I deal on N.Korea etc?"

Because Trump is Trump, he was totally for leaks before he was against them. Like the entire GOP, Trump was giddy over the Democratic Party emails leaked by Wikileaks (now determined to have been working with Russian intelligence to undermine the US elections). At one point he openly invited Russia to hack Hillary Clinton: "Russia, if you're listening, I hope you're able to find the thirty thousand emails that are missing . . . They probably have them. I'd like to have them released."

But, of course, now that he is the target—and true to standard-issue GOP hypocrisy—his tune has changed. Yesterday, leaks were cool; today, leaks are "un-American."

It's not just government agencies that have the goods on Trump's inner workings. The voice recording of Trump bragging about sexually assaulting women by "grab[bing] them by the pussy" was itself a leak from somewhere inside *Access Hollywood*. Given Trump's extensive media appearances throughout the decades, there are reams of additional incriminating material just waiting to see the light of day.

Financial institutions have copies of Trump documents, including tax returns, that should be available for public review. Eric Trump, son of the president, warned that leaking his father's returns would be "dangerous" and "third world," reinforcing how scared they are of this actually happening. "When personal information is put out by people for political agendas, as a civilian, it's actually scary," he said, forgetting that his father is no longer a civilian.

The Freedom of the Press Foundation has tips on how to securely blow your whistle, assuming you have a real tip, backed by real evidence.

1. **Leak to the right organizations.** If your tip concerns Trump regime wrongdoing at the local level, target local media. If it's at higher levels, go with the big DC-based media outlets (the *New York Times*, the *Washington Post*) and investigative journalism organizations (like ProPublica). Look to see which individual journalists are focused on your material. For example, David Fahrenthold of the *Washington Post* won a Pulitzer in 2017 for his deep (and lonely) dive into Trump's finances during the

2016 campaign. He'd be a safe bet. Send to more than one source to improve chances of publication.

2. **Be cautious.** Don't call or email from work. Stay off your work-issued communications devices. Make sure the tipping material can't be traced back to you (as in, you're the only person who would know), or if it can, be prepared for the consequences. Don't tell anyone you are leaking, except perhaps a lawyer; those communications are protected. Make sure that if you leak digital documents, there is no file metadata that can give you away. You can google for metadata-removing apps, or take a screenshot of the file from your computer, as that strips away most incriminating metadata.

3. **Minimize risk.** Send materials through physical mail, and don't use a return address that can be traced back to you. The US Post Office takes exterior pictures of all mail. Mail from a sidewalk mailbox location far from yours, so the USPS origin stamp doesn't give hints to your location. Use burner phones, the prepaid kind that can't be traced back to you, and pay with cash. Follow the procedures for security detailed in chapter 10, like using Signal for text messaging. If leaking electronically, make sure the news organization has a secure, encrypted document dump. SecureDrop, used by the *New York Times*, the *Washington Post*, BuzzFeed, and ProPublica (among others), ensures that even the news agency doesn't know who is dropping off the documents unless you choose to tell them.

Most of us don't have access to incriminating information about Trump or his cronies. But for those of you who do, you're sitting on a gold mine. Leak it! Whether you out yourself or not, you will be a national hero. Just be thoughtful, and take appropriate steps to responsibly protect yourself and your family.

22

OBSTRUCT, DELAY, STYMIE

RECOMMENDED RESOURCES

Muck Rock FOIA
Public Citizen, "How to File a FOIA Request"
RulesatRisk.org
United to Protect Democracy

IT'S TRUE, ELECTIONS decide who is in power. And that power is seemingly unchecked if, as in the current situation, one party controls the White House, Congress, and the Supreme Court. However, even the governing trifecta does not give the ruling party dictatorial powers, and there are mechanisms in place to stymie, delay, and bedevil Republican efforts. So not only can you rage against the machine; you might be able to help grind its gears to a halt.

WHEN BUREAUCRACY IS YOUR FRIEND

Take the regulatory process, for example. When Congress passes a bill and the president signs it into law, the executive branch is charged with implementing that law (including interpreting it how they see fit—subject to judicial review). The relevant agencies then issue regulations detailing how the law will be carried out and enforced; legislation is generally a blueprint, not a step-by-step how-to. And that regulatory process offers incredible opportunities to influence, delay, and obstruct the final outcome.

For example, the Environmental Protection Agency was tasked with promulgating new formaldehyde emissions standards in 2010. Yet thanks to industry pressure, the regulation wasn't finalized until December 2016. The Occupational Safety and Health Administration began work regulating exposure to crystalline silica in 2003 yet didn't issue final rules until this year, 2017, and even now, the rules are currently being delayed to offer employers more education and guidance.

Those same processes available to corporate influencers are available to us. We can tie up much of the GOP's destructive agenda in the bureaucracy. Even noncontroversial regulations require a year to promulgate. Controversial ones—and there will be plenty of those—can be delayed long enough to be abandoned by the next Democratic administration in 2021.

So how can we use the regulatory process as a delay tactic? First of all, all regulations allow for a public comment period, typically lasting several months; agencies are required to respond to comments. Once the comment period closes, the rules are subject to judicial challenge—which can further drag things out. Furthermore, regulatory agencies are required to conduct cost-benefit analyses (a GOP ploy to delay regulations that impact big corporations, which we can now use to our advantage), and on many types of regulations, additional public input is required after that analysis.

Issue advocacy organizations will be well attuned to these opportunities, will instruct their members when public comment periods open, and will offer arguments to make—essentially finding legal flaws in the proposed regulations, as well as raising unforeseen costs. If the agency does not properly address those concerns, those groups can use that opening as the basis for administrative and legal challenges. And the more people comment, the greater the media coverage the rule will receive, which will make the impacted agency even more gun-shy and careful, causing even more delay. So when the opportunity arises and your favorite advocacy groups alert you to an open public comment period . . . make a comment!

FREEDOM, MEET YOUR FRIEND, INFORMATION

The Freedom of Information Act (FOIA), long used by media to try to hold government officials and agencies accountable, has been weaponized by the Right, who use it to tie up Democratic administrations with reams of information requests to delay and obstruct their work. "We're pushing three-quarters of a million" FOIA requests each year, said Fred J. Sadler, who handled FOIA operations for the US Food and Drug Administration during the Obama administration. "You just don't have enough resources."

Turnabout is fair play, so it behooves Resistance fighters to return the favor. The easiest way to do this is by supporting liberal groups and media organizations like the Reporters Committee for Freedom of the Press; you might even file some of those FOIA requests yourself. If you are an attorney, consider supporting FOIA lawsuits pro bono. The

Trump regime will slow-walk answering those requests, so legal challenges will be critical in demanding proper government transparency.

DON'T IGNORE YOUR STATE'S ROLE

While the opportunities for legislative public hearings are scarce at the federal level, that is not the case at the state and local levels. It was at the state level that Republicans instituted the voting restrictions that helped deliver Michigan, Ohio, Pennsylvania, and Wisconsin to Trump. Make your presence seen and heard at your state capitol and city halls. Attend and participate in hearings—both on offense, pushing for legislation that furthers the progressive agenda, and on defense, preventing further rollbacks of rights and benefits.

AND THOSE SENATE DEMOCRATS . . .

Even with a truncated filibuster, Democrats in the Senate minority have incredible power to stop the GOP's agenda dead in its tracks. What they lack, as usual, is the will. By some counts, there are around 1,200 executive-branch nominees requiring Senate approval, each potentially requiring *four* days of debate to confirm. That includes such positions as the intellectual property enforcement coordinator at the Office of Management and Budget.

Senate Democrats can drag out each one of those nominations; delay long enough, and it would take the entire term just to get through the process. So let's delay! Trump himself has been slow to offer nominations, giving Democrats more opportunities to take up valuable time demanding a full debate for even the most harmless appointees, like members of the National Museum and Library Services Board.

Using appointees to delay Senate business is great, but Democrats have an even better weapon at their disposal: they can weaponize "unanimous consent," the parliamentary procedure used to speed through routine Senate business. Regular Senate procedures require up to seven days to pass legislation, assuming there are no amendments—each of which would drag out the process further. By refusing to provide unanimous consent to speed up the process, senators can dramatically bog down the chamber. There are additional tools, like quorum calls, that your senators can use to gum up the works through unanimous consent rules. Pressure your senators to do so at every opportunity.

The beauty of the unanimous consent rule is that it's applied literally: it requires *unanimous* consent. All it takes is one senator on the floor to object to consent. It's what Democrats should've done to block the Gorsuch nomination to the Supreme Court, and it's what they should do moving forward to minimize the threat of right-wing Trumpist-Republican governance. A single rejection of unanimous consent can delay Senate business for days; as long as the GOP controls the Senate, our motto should be "Less is more."

And don't worry about any potential political fallout from following the path of relentless obstruction—Republicans pioneered these tactics. The voting public doesn't give a damn.

23

POLITICIZE CONSUMERISM

RECOMMENDED RESOURCES

EndCitizensUnited.org
FollowtheMoney.org
JusticeDemocrats.com
LegalDesign.org
OpenSecrets.org

WE ALL KNOW by now that corporations impact the political process. Yes, it's true, corporate money distorts our politics and can benefit certain moneyed interests. And it's true that those outcomes can lead to disaster, such as the banking collapse at the end of George W. Bush's presidential term. But it's also true that attacking "corporations" on the whole, as if they're all part of a single monolithic category, is overly simplistic. Frankly, it can be counterproductive.

Many corporations were strong backers of marriage equality efforts across the country. The corporate community in North Carolina viciously attacked the state GOP's efforts to discriminate against the LGBTQ community. And even when they're bad, like General Electric's Jeffrey Immelt's support of climate change denier Scott Pruitt to run the Environmental Protection Agency, they can sometimes be good, like when he criticized the Muslim travel ban.

CORPORATIONS AREN'T PEOPLE—BUT PEOPLE ARE CORPORATIONS

Within this vast gray area of corporate participation in our politics, there are real opportunities for the Resistance to further our agenda. In the age of social media, it is absurdly easy to impact a company's brand and reputation and force them to take sides in public policy battles. And the fact is, on almost every issue, the majority of the American people (and particularly the largest consumers of the products and services corporations offer) stand with us.

Outside of the most naturally conservative industries like fossil fuel extraction, gun manufacturing, and the military-industrial complex, there are real opportunities to use some political jujitsu to turn the power of corporate influence to our benefit. Earlier, we discussed the power and effectiveness of boycotts, but leveraging corporate behavior for positive change doesn't always have to be confrontational.

Corporate America is highly attuned to our nation's cultural and demographic shifts; their profits and growth depend on it. They don't benefit from alienating potential customers. They also can't attract the best and brightest employees if their values preach exclusion. In fact, according to top corporate consulting firms like McKinsey, employees' concerns about workplace diversity, equality, and sustainability are among the most powerful drivers of corporate change. In the September 2008 edition of *McKinsey Quarterly*, they note:

> *The war for talent today is truly global, so recruiting and retaining a diverse workforce is a more competitive business issue than ever . . . It's important for a company's workforce to not only reflect the diversity of talent available in the world today but also to mirror the diversity of its customer base.*

No human resources expert has ever suggested banning brown people with funny-sounding names as a smart recruiting strategy. And so corporations are among the first to suffer when Republicans enact oppressive and transparently racist policies like the travel ban.

CORPORATE AMERICA IS HIGHLY ATTUNED TO OUR NATION'S CULTURAL AND DEMOGRAPHIC SHIFTS. THEY DON'T BENEFIT FROM ALIENATING POTENTIAL CUSTOMERS. THEY ALSO CAN'T ATTRACT THE BEST AND BRIGHTEST EMPLOYEES IF THEIR VALUES PREACH EXCLUSION.

TRAVEL AGENTS: NOT FOND OF TRAVEL BANS

Companies focused on the tourism industry are already being devastated by the anti-American sentiment being stoked, worldwide, by Trump's revanchist approach to foreign business and tourism visitors, let alone immigrants. Talk to any foreigner who's come to the US since Trump's nomination, and they'll tell you: immigration authorities are not exactly rolling out the welcome mat.

According to travel-booking app Hopper, searches for US flights from around the world were down since the 2016 election, significantly so in many places (like China, where they were down 40 percent). The one exception: Russia. (Go figure.) The tourism slump affects US airlines, hotels, car rental outfits, and the millions of Americans and legal residents who make a living off tourism.

But it's not just the tourism industry that loses under Trumpism. The sustainable energy industry is also under threat, even though it employs significantly more people than coal—4.5 million jobs versus 76,000. That puts coal in the same league as . . . the bowling industry (69,000 jobs).

So every company negatively impacted by Trump and the GOP, whether in tourism, clean energy, or tech, is a potential ally in the coming battles. It doesn't help us to be reflexively anti-corporate.

THE KIDS ARE ALL RIGHT

On the other side of the corporate equation, of course, are the rest of us: no company can exist without customers who want to pay for its product or service. While members of *Daily Kos* and ProgressNow skew heavily toward the justice side of the consumer equation, there are also deeper demographic shifts occurring, reflected in consumer habits, that bode well for the Resistance, and are a nightmare for Trump and the GOP.

It turns out that, for all the condescension they receive, millennial consumers, in particular, are heavily value-driven in their purchasing decisions. "Affiliation with a cause is more important to the Millennial generation than to any previous generation," concluded a study by marketing firm Barkley. "That means, as a brand that is searching for ways to engage and tap into this next generation of consumers, showing them that you care is critical." The study also found that millennials are far more social consumers; they care what other people think and make their purchases accordingly.

That's why the most forward-thinking corporations are resisting major tenets of the Trump agenda with little prompting from activists. They're doing it because it makes business sense. For example, over one hundred major companies, including Apple, Facebook, Google, Microsoft, and Tesla, signed an amicus brief in opposition to Trump's Muslim travel ban; going one better, Starbucks announced a plan to hire ten thousand refugees at its stores around the world. Outraged conservatives (including Trump himself) promised a Starbucks boycott in response; as of this writing, there's no indication of a negative impact on Starbucks' profits. (Trump loses. Again.)

For its part, Lyft donated $1 million to the ACLU, partially because it's the right thing to do, but also because it helped Lyft differentiate itself from its larger (but now besieged) competitor. Uber, the bête noir of the tech industry, crossed the proverbial picket lines during the JFK airport taxi strike, which taxi drivers called to show solidarity with Muslim ban protesters inside JFK. Uber CEO Travis Kalanick responded to the backlash by quitting Trump's CEO advisory board.

So what can we do to mobilize these corporations on our behalf?

1. **Shy away from cartoonish demonization of corporations.** We know it's easier to rail against "neoliberal" corporate influence, but the reality is that corporate America is like the humans who build and run those companies—some are good, some are bad, and some are . . . complicated. Focus your ire on Koch Industries, not potential allies.

2. **Boycott!** It's effective, and brands are responsive to the negative

PR of a boycott. Also, make sure you spread the word about your boycotting on social media, so the targeted companies hear about it. Most large companies employ "social listening" tools to keep track of what's being said about them in order to gauge when and how to respond. Companies are just as worried about impacts on their brand and consumer perceptions as they are about material impacts on their sales.

3. **Oppose *Citizens United*.** The *Citizens United* Supreme Court decision gave corporations the same First Amendment rights as *people*, which is not just ludicrous on its face but legally incoherent. When's the last time you saw a corporation jailed for breaking a law? As is, corporations get all the benefits of personhood with none of the responsibilities. Corporate spending should be disclosed and limits should be enforced. End Citizens United is doing great work organizing to this end.

4. **Spend according to your values.** Spend money on values-driven companies like Seventh Generation, Patagonia, Burt's Bees, and Method. Ditch your gas guzzler altogether if you can; look into electric cars (battery ranges are increasing while prices are dropping). Remember, a portion of every dollar you give to a gas station goes to fund Republican politicians. If you own your own roof, get solar panels installed. Avoid companies that fund the right-wing machine, such as anything made by Koch Industries. If you have a local credit union, do your banking there instead of at one of the major too-big-to-fail banks like Bank of America or Wells Fargo. Look into cutting the television cord so you can ditch your cable provider. (Alternatives for Internet access, however, remain scarce.) Shop locally when possible.

5. **Demand diversity.** The smartest companies know that they can attract the best talent, and sell to the largest market, only if their

staff reflects our nation's demographics. Another McKinsey study found a statistically significant relationship between companies with women and people of color in their upper ranks and higher earnings. Not only is this diversity good for a company's bottom line, it also economically empowers marginalized communities and erodes the institutional racism and bigotry that have perpetuated our sad history of repression.

The fight for our country has drawn myriad battle lines, and they crisscross corporate America like a hashtag. Resist the urge to paint all of corporate America with a single brush, and instead work to cultivate our natural allies while neutering our opponents.

24

FIGHT FOR JUSTICE

RECOMMENDED RESOURCES

Anti-Defamation League
BlackLivesMatter.com
CivilRights.org
ColorofChange.org
JustLeadershipUSA.org
Mexican American Legal Defense and Education Fund
NAACP.org
SentencingProject.org
ShowingUpforRacialJustice.org

OUR CRIMINAL JUSTICE system is designed to reinforce a structure of privilege that has created gross inequities between white communities and those of color; our "centrist" media reinforces this bias by following the law enforcement community's lead in how they portray different types of crime.

THE RESISTANCE HANDBOOK: 45 WAYS TO FIGHT TRUMP

Want proof? Consider how the crack epidemic in inner cities was considered a "criminal" problem. Yet somehow the current opioid epidemic in rural, white America is considered a "public health crisis." The message couldn't be more clear: to America's criminal justice system, people of color are criminals; white people are victims.

The entire "war on drugs" is an abject failure, but embedded within that failure is an even deeper injustice: due largely to the way we've criminalized substance abuse, there are 2.2 million people in America's prisons today, according to the International Centre for Prison Studies. That's over six hundred people per hundred thousand, the largest incarceration rate—by far—of any nation on the planet. Second-place Russia lags far behind, at just over four hundred people per hundred thousand.

And that prison inmate population doesn't even reflect the reality of an equal distribution of incidence of crime across the American population. Just one in seventeen white men will end up in prison, while the number is one in *three* among black men, and one in six among Latino men, according to the Bureau of Justice Statistics. Similarly, while just one in one hundred and eleven white women will end up in prison, that number is one in eighteen for black women and one in forty-five for Latinas.

THE CRIME: BREATHING WHILE BLACK

It's not as if we don't have a robust body of evidence of the systemic nature of racial profiling in the United States. Across the spectrum and across the years, justice and civil rights experts have found incontrovertible proof that the American system of criminal justice has substantial racial bias and is in need of urgent reform.

- A 2015 University of California–Davis study by Professor Cody T. Ross found "evidence of a significant bias in the killing of unarmed black Americans relative to unarmed white Americans, in that the probability of being black, unarmed, and shot by police is about 3.49 times the probability of being white, unarmed, and shot by police on average." The study also found no correlation between crime rates and the rates of police shootings. In other words, the bias was wholly accounted for by race. An April 2016 *Washington Post* analysis found "the only thing that was significant in predicting whether someone shot and killed by police was unarmed was whether or not they were black . . . Crime variables did not matter in terms of predicting whether the person killed was unarmed."

- African-Americans are also far more likely to be stopped by police. According to the San Francisco district attorney's office, "although Black people accounted for less than 15 percent of all stops in 2015, they accounted for over 42 percent of all non-consent searches following stops."

- A March 2015 Justice Department investigation of the police department in Ferguson, Missouri, in the wake of the Michael Brown shooting found that "African Americans are more than twice as likely as white drivers to be searched during vehicle stops even after controlling for non-race based variables such as the reason the vehicle stop was initiated, but are found in possession of contraband 26% less often than white drivers, suggesting officers are impermissibly considering race as a factor when determining whether to search."

- In Chicago, an April 2016 police accountability report found that "black and Hispanic drivers were searched approximately four times as often as white drivers, yet [the Chicago Police

Department's] own data show that contraband was found on white drivers twice as often as black and Hispanic drivers."

- A July 2014 National Institute of Justice study found that African-Americans in New York City were more likely to sit in jail while awaiting trial (disrupting family life and employment) than whites, who could better afford to pay for bail. The study also showed that in New York, after controlling for the severity of the crime and prior record, blacks were 13 percent more likely to be offered a plea deal that included jail time.
- A 2014 study from the University of Michigan Law School by Sonja B. Starr and M. Marit Rehavi found that prison sentences for black defendants in federal courts were 10 percent longer than those of whites, once again controlling for the severity of the crime and prior record, and that prosecutors were twice as likely to file charges against black defendants that carry mandatory minimum sentences as whites.
- The "school to prison" pipeline criminalizes school misbehavior. According to 2012 data from the Department of Education, 40 percent of students expelled from US schools each year are black, and 70 percent of incidents leading to arrests involve blacks or Latinos.

JEFFERSON BEAUREGARD SESSIONS: A REAL THREAT

President Barack Obama's Justice Department was working toward addressing many of these inequities. For example, Attorney General Eric Holder charged Maricopa County's odious former sheriff Joe Arpaio with criminal contempt for refusing to stop his long history of racially charged policing. However, thanks to Donald Trump's presidency—and his appointment of notorious racist Jeff Sessions as attorney general—all such progress is halted.

Sessions has never been shy about his racism, and the African-American community has never been shy about calling him out on his racism. When Ronald Reagan tried to appoint Sessions to a lifetime judgeship, Coretta Scott King, Martin Luther King's widow, wrote:

> *The irony of Mr. Sessions' nomination is that, if con-firmed, he will be given a life tenure for doing with a federal prosecution what the local sheriffs accomplished twenty years ago with clubs and cattle prods . . . I believe his confirmation would have a devastating effect on not only the judicial system in Alabama, but also on the prog-ress we have made toward fulfilling my husband's dream.*

Already, Sessions has ordered a "sweeping review of police reform" initiated under Obama with the obvious intent to halt such reforms. He also attempted to block implementation of a consent decree requiring reform of Baltimore's police department. When a judge shot him down, Sessions said the move would result in a "less safe city." Amazingly, both Baltimore's mayor *and* its police commissioner disagreed.

So what can we do to fight for an equitable society, particularly in the face of a Republican Party hell-bent on going back to the glory days of the Jim Crow South?

1. **Support national organizations** like the NAACP, the Anti-Defamation League, the Mexican American Legal Defense and Educational Fund (MALDEF), and Black Lives Matter. While the ACLU has riled communities of color with its sup-port for Breitbart neo-Nazi racists like Milo Yiannopoulos on

free-speech grounds, they also have focused extensively on justice issues. These organizations will send alerts related to public comments (on regulatory matters), phone call efforts, and other actions.

2. **Pay attention to district attorney races.** District attorneys are at the forefront of justice issues, deciding which cases to pursue, what charges to file, and what sentences to recommend. They can either protect police departments or hold them accountable. They lives of defendants are literally in their hands.

3. **Organize locally.** Most policy that directly impacts your community is developed at the local level. Most law enforcement you will interact with is either local or state. District attorneys are local. Most criminal law and sentencing guidelines are state and local. Sheriffs are local. In fact, one of Sessions' goals during his tenure will be to remove all federal oversight of the local criminal enforcement system. Thus, our most important victories (or losses) will come at the local level. This is where the biggest fights will be waged.

Conservatives are heavily invested in perpetuating our current, overtly racist system of justice. To them, it's not broken: it's working exactly as intended. By fighting for a just and equitable society, we are working toward an America that treats everyone the same, not just the privileged few.

FIGHT FOR LGBTQ RIGHTS

RECOMMENDED RESOURCES

CampusPride.org
EqualityFederation.org
GLSEN.org
LambdaLegal.org
PFLAG.org
National Center for Lesbian Rights
TransgenderLawCenter.org

IN AN ELECTION year full of weirdness, North Carolina stood out in particular. Its Republican governor, Pat McCrory, along with his GOP-dominated legislature, declared all-out war on the progressive coalition, with its primary target the state's LGBTQ community.

North Carolina's House Bill 2, rammed through the state legislature during a hastily called special session, banned any local nondiscrimination protections on the basis of sexual orientation and gender identity and prohibited transgender individuals from using bathrooms that did not match the gender assigned to them at birth.

The legislature had sprung into frenzied action because Charlotte, the state's largest city (and a Democratic stronghold), had passed a local ordinance that aimed to protect LGBTQ people from discrimination. It turns out the same conservatives who love to bray about "local control" when it suits their interests can't abide when that control violates their bigoted preferences. Besides, take away discrimination against people you don't like, and what's left of conservatism besides tax cuts for the wealthy? You don't win elections appealing only to the 1 percent.

The law was bitterly opposed by North Carolina's business community (see chapter 23), who were mortified by seeing their state branded as a champion of bigotry. Heavyweight artists like Bruce Springsteen canceled concerts, top-tier companies like PayPal withdrew job-creating investments, and in the biggest blow by far, the NCAA pulled all collegiate sports tournaments from the state, including the Tar Heels' beloved March Madness basketball games. "Our future as Americans should be focused on inclusion and prosperity, and not discrimination and division," Apple declared shortly after McCrory signed the bill. "We were disappointed to see Governor McCrory sign this legislation."

PAWNS IN THE CULTURE WARS

But Republicans were elated. Not only was their prerogative to discriminate maintained, but the new law was signed in March of an election year. They had a divisive social issue on which to campaign for the November elections. Many Democrats fretted that liberals, once again, were pushing their party outside the mainstream, that society wasn't quite ready to accept transgender individuals.

And yet when the dust cleared that November, after Donald Trump had carried the state by three points, it was McCrory himself who took the fall. Democrat Roy Cooper, who as state attorney general had refused to defend the discriminatory law in court, ran against McCrory and won by making his principled opposition to HB 2 the centerpiece of his campaign. The law was so toxic that even a slice of *Trump voters* thought it had gone too far.

In a night full of pain and misery, Cooper's victory showed that Democrats who stood strong against discrimination—alongside some of the most marginalized people in our country—could, and did, win.

But other Republicans didn't take McCrory's loss as a sign; rather, they've picked up right where North Carolina left off and are trying to pass these so-called bathroom bills in more than a dozen states across the country. Trump himself has boosted the effort by rescinding Obama administration policies that encourage schools to let transgender students use whichever bathroom or locker room is consistent with their gender. Trump also reversed an Obama executive order requiring federal contractors to adopt nondiscrimination protections for their gay and transgender workers (though federal contractors are still prohibited from discriminating against LGBTQ employees via a separate order).

Meanwhile, any hopes LGBTQ Americans had of being explicitly counted in the 2020 US Census were dashed when the Census Bureau announced it would not include proposed questions about sexual orientation and gender identity in the upcoming survey. These moves were deliberate efforts "to erase LGBTQ people from federal data used to inform budgets and policies across the government," said Chad Griffin, the president of the Human Rights Campaign. "Their intent is clear. By denying we exist, the Trump administration hopes to deny us equality."

THE RESISTANCE HANDBOOK: 45 WAYS TO FIGHT TRUMP

Given that the Trump regime is replete with antigay activists, these moves should be no surprise. Vice President Mike Pence made himself a national star with the GOP faithful by signing an anti-LGBTQ "license to discriminate" bill into law while he was governor of Indiana. Attorney General Jeff Sessions, never one to miss an opportunity to institutionalize hate, advocated for a constitutional ban on same-sex marriages; Education Secretary Betsy DeVos, a billionaire donor to antigay causes, is a champion of "conversion therapy" (which aims to turn gay people straight); and James Renne, a Trump transition official who ended up with a senior role at the Department of Agriculture, literally purged the George W. Bush administration of gay employees.

So yes, the Trump White House crowd will be gunning for the rights of the LGBTQ community. So what can we do to resist?

1. **Take a stand for LGBTQ rights.** Conservatives want to drive nonstraight folks back into the shadows, strip away recognition, pretend they don't exist. Any effort in support of this community starts by showing solidarity and support for our allies in the LGBTQ community, recognizing the struggles they face, and being willing to stand up for their rights—whether you're marching in the streets or sitting in a boardroom.

2. **Support national organizations** like Lambda Legal, the Transgender Law Center, and other groups fighting for LGBTQ rights. Not only are these groups on the front lines of the equality battle, but they will keep you apprised of ways you can engage in the fight, from making phone calls to rallying in support of LGBTQ individuals.

3. **Organize locally.** As North Carolina shows, states and local jurisdictions are on the front lines in the battle for equality. Lobby your elected officials to pass antidiscrimination

ordinances and laws, and remain vigilant to ensure that they are properly enforced. Fight attempts to legislate bigotry. Join local groups focused on these issues to keep yourself properly informed.

4. **Realize that the LGBTQ fight is a winner!** While standing up for LGBTQ issues has long been seen as a righteous stance by most progressives, it was often viewed as a losing strategy politically. Anyone still operating under this assumption is doing LGBTQ Americans and the greater progressive cause a disservice. Indeed, what their movement has accomplished in the last decade alone is truly awe inspiring. McCrory's ouster in an election year full of Democratic defeats is the perfect case in point: blatantly targeting gay and transgender Americans is now a political loser, even in a swing state—but it wasn't just a dozen years ago. Conservatives know this, which is why they are cloaking many of their discriminatory efforts in the language of "religious freedom." Recognizing what LGBTQ Americans have accomplished as individuals and as a community—and working to replicate those lessons wherever possible in other movements—is the best resistance possible.

Conservatives are heavily invested in rolling back gains made by the LGBTQ community and in resisting further attempts at true equality. It is critical, for their core ideology, that white, straight men continue to control the levers of power. Thus it is up to us to resist, ensuring that all of us, regardless of who we love, have an equal shot at life, liberty, and the pursuit of happiness.

26

RESIST THE GOP WAR ON WOMEN

RECOMMENDED RESOURCES

LVW.org
MomsRising.org
Now.org
PlannedParenthoodAction.org
ProChoiceAmerica.org
VoteProChoice.us
WeAreUltraviolet.org

DAYS AFTER HIS inauguration, popular-vote loser Donald Trump sparked his war on women's rights by signing an executive order reinstating the "global gag rule." The rule—cooked up by right-wing fundamentalist radicals (like Vice President Pence)—prohibits the US from funding *any* international organizations that offer or advise women on family planning and reproductive health options if they include abortion advice or services.

Radical Christianists, who have more in common with Taliban values than American ones, have been trying to eviscerate women's right to control their own bodies for decades; in keeping with their sharia-esque view of the world, Trump signed the order surrounded by seven smiling white Christian men.

People were suitably outraged, of course. "As long as you live you'll never see a photograph of 7 women signing legislation about what men can do with their reproductive organs," read one tweet. But no one was surprised. This is, after all, the same Trump who bragged about sexually assaulting women by "grab[bing] them by the pussy." It was Trump who said, "26,000 unreported sexual assaults in the military . . . What did these geniuses expect when they put men & women together?"

Trump's disdain and lack of respect for women has been well publicized. He's the guy who called Rosie O'Donnell "disgusting," "a slob," "a big fat pig," and "a very unattractive person." It was Trump who, according to reporting by the *New York Times*, allowed only "the most attractive women" at the Trump Organization to take lunch orders. "That was purely about looks," a former construction executive who worked with Trump told the newspaper. "He wanted the people in that room to think that all the women who worked for him were beautiful."

Ultimately, a woman doesn't have value for Trump unless she's young and "hot" (or his daughter Ivanka). As he himself said, "It doesn't really matter what [the media] write as long as you've got a young and beautiful piece of ass."

TRUMP REALLY IS THE GOP'S DADDY

It was inevitable that Republicans would eventually embrace a rank misogynist like Trump given their long-standing views on the role of women in society. This isn't a party with a history of respecting women's equal role in government, or their freedom as individuals to make their own choices. Of the 10 people in the GOP's Senate and House leadership, only one is a woman. Of the 104 women currently serving in Congress, just 26 are Republican.

The GOP's antiwoman agenda extends deep into policy, beyond their hostility toward reproductive rights. Trump and Republican House speaker Paul Ryan's first attempt at an Obamacare replacement plan explicitly excluded women's reproductive health services from coverage, including pre- and postnatal care. The Republican approach to family planning is basically this: HAVE THE BABY! Just don't expect any help in properly caring for yourself and the baby, before or after they're born.

Given their open hostility toward women's health care, one could be forgiven for concluding that Republicans just don't understand much about the female body. Remember, this is the party of Todd Akin, the 2012 Missouri Senate candidate who responded to a question about abortions for pregnancies caused by rape, "If it's a legitimate rape, the female body has ways to try to shut that whole thing down."

> **GIVEN THEIR OPEN HOSTILITY TOWARD WOMEN'S HEALTH CARE, ONE COULD BE FORGIVEN FOR CONCLUDING THAT REPUBLICANS JUST DON'T UNDERSTAND MUCH ABOUT THE FEMALE BODY.**

And for a party that pretends to care so much about babies, they sure have zero interest in lending a supporting hand. For example, on the floor of the US House, Illinois Republican John Shimkus complained about Obamacare's mandated care provisions. When asked which mandated services, exactly, he objected to, he replied, "What about men having to purchase prenatal care?" Answering a similar question, Kansas senator Pat Roberts responded, condescendingly, "I wouldn't want to lose my mammograms." During a 2013 debate, North Carolina Republican representative Renee Ellmers once sneered, "To the best of your knowledge, has a man ever delivered a baby?" If it doesn't belong to a man, these Republicans can't fathom why they should care.

But Trump's assault on women's health was just the opening salvo in the burgeoning Republican war on women. Soon after taking office, he also overturned two key regulations: one mandating wage transparency, allowing women to ensure they are receiving equal pay for equal work, and the other barring forced arbitration for sexual harassment cases—or as they're known, "cover-up clauses." White women still earn just eighty cents to every dollar a man receives, adding up to $1 million over a forty-year career—a $1 million "woman tax" that Republicans are fighting to perpetuate. Black women and Latinas make even less— yet another way people of color are economically disempowered.

So how can we fight back?

1. **Support pro-women organizations** at the national level such as NARAL, EMILY's List, NOW, and Planned Parenthood.

2. **Encourage political engagement.** According to exit polls, single women supported Hillary Clinton by a margin of 63–32 in the 2016 presidential election, while married women supported Clinton just 49–47. Other polls confirm this "marriage gap" among women. Interestingly, it doesn't matter if "unmarried" refers to a young single woman, a divorcee, or a widow. A woman becomes more Republican when married and reverts to being a Democrat if newly single. Problem is, married women vote

at much higher rates than unmarried women. The Voter Participation Center found that in "the 2014 election, unmarried women were a slim minority of vote-eligible women—but only cast two-thirds as many votes as married women." If unmarried women voted at the same levels as married women that year, nearly 9 million additional women would've voted. Preliminary data from the 2016 elections suggests little has changed.

3. **Act in solidarity with women organizers.** Critics (mostly men) originally claimed the postinauguration Women's March would be unnecessarily exclusionary. Instead, it turned into the nation's largest protest in its history. By showing up in force, regardless of gender, the Resistance demonstrated unyielding solidarity with the women's agenda.

4. **Put women in charge.** Our movement is majority female, and yet their ranks are underrepresented in our organizations. Our movement's leadership must reflect our movement's demographics. Period.

5. **Fight locally.** Conservatives have waged relentless local campaigns to limit the rights of women, from abortion, to family and paid sick leave, to equal pay. Engage in your state and municipal governments to support good policy, block the bad stuff, and cultivate the political women leaders of tomorrow. The deeper our bench, the easier it will be to elect women at higher levels. And let's face it, even *Republican women* are better than their male counterparts. The path toward better government requires electing more women.

6. **Empower mothers.** Rather than protect and celebrate motherhood, Republicans often use a woman's parenthood status to further discriminate against her in employment, housing, and government services. Note how Republicans are fighting

to eliminate pre- and postnatal care from the list of required services by health insurers. "Recent research . . . shows that even when women maintain their professional ambitions, motherhood often triggers strong and blatant workplace bias," wrote the *Harvard Business Review*.

7. **Educate yourself and share knowledge.** Many issues may appear to apply to everyone equally, but on closer investigation may disproportionately affect women. For example, victims of domestic violence who report the crime often face eviction from landlords who penalize them for being part of a "domestic disturbance" drawing the attention of law enforcement.

Republicans have a vested interest in protecting the economic power and social perks they, as white, straight men, receive by virtue of birthright and institutionalized misogyny. They see full equality for women as a threat to their power; it's our job to carry through on that threat and empower women everywhere.

27

FIGHT FOR THE COURTS

RECOMMENDED RESOURCES

American Constitutional Society
BrennanCenter.org
United to Protect Democracy

AS AN ILLEGITIMATE president, Donald Trump should never have been allowed to nominate, let alone confirm, newly minted Supreme Court justice Neil Gorsuch. But the GOP's undermining of our judicial system didn't begin with Trump, Gorsuch, or the blocking of Obama nominee Merrick Garland last year; in fact, their long-term commitment to stacking the courts with extreme right-wing judges is perhaps the greatest threat we face as a nation.

The Gorsuch appointment was the culmination of a GOP strategy to deny the confirmation of hundreds of Obama's judicial picks, denying the legitimacy of Democratic governance, even when we win elections.

Republicans filibustered 20 of Obama's federal district court judge nominees; prior to the Obama presidency, only 17 had been filibustered in the entire history of the nation. After taking control of the Senate in 2015, Republicans confirmed just 11 judges, the lowest number since 1960. In total, fewer judges were approved during the last two years of Obama's presidency than at any point since the 1897–98 session—and at the time there were just 25 circuit court judges, compared to 179 today. In the end, there were 87 federal judicial vacancies left unfilled at the end of Obama's term, including seven appeals court seats, despite nominees awaiting confirmation for 61 of them.

And, of course, they refused to consider Obama's nomination of Merrick Garland to the Supreme Court for almost a year, riding out the clock until a new administration could come in. When it looked like Hillary Clinton would win the White House, conservatives like the Heritage Foundation and Senator Ted Cruz argued that the court could operate fine with eight justices, vowing to block any Clinton nominee for the entirety of her term. Other Republicans argued that "the people" should decide who got to fill that seat. And then, when the people decided they wanted Hillary Clinton, the will of the voter was no longer important.

But their bet had paid off. With Trump in the White House, it was okay again for the high court to have nine justices.

Trump may have gotten Gorsuch confirmed, but there was one hugely positive outcome of that battle—the core of the Democratic caucus held together, proving that they were ready and willing to present a unified front against future Republican nominees. These empty seats belong to us, and Senate Democrats need to make sure to fight like hell to keep them open until we have a legitimate, popularly elected president.

1. **Urge Democratic senators to obstruct.** Pundits and politicians fret that the voting public will punish a party for overly obstructing a president's agenda. The last eight years proved otherwise. The voting public was oblivious to the obstruction. Meanwhile, conservatives rewarded their obstructionist senators, fighting hard for those who fought for them. The same lesson applies today—the Resistance will fight hard for Democrats that they see fighting for them. And when it comes to Trump's judicial appointments, the only acceptable answer is no.

2. **Urge Democratic senators to obstruct, part 2.** As we mentioned earlier in this book, Democrats can make use of the "unanimous consent" rule to slow Senate business to a crawl. If Republicans insist on filling these empty seats, Democrats should block even the most routine of Senate business, requiring time-consuming quorum calls and votes. Republicans may still win those votes when the clock runs out, but they will have wasted a great deal of precious time doing so.

3. **Call, call, call.** Democrats need to be reminded to stand firm against any Trump judges. Republicans are looking at the Resistance with trepidation, and moderate Republicans are particularly skittish. They held strong on the Gorsuch nomination, but will their resolve hold the closer we get to elections?

4. **Win elections!** The Senate map is brutal for Democrats in 2018 and much more favorable in 2020. It doesn't matter. Given national sentiment, we have an outside chance of winning the chamber during the midterm elections. So if you live in a Senate battleground state, gear up, organize, and get ready to volunteer. If you don't, get ready to help our allies in those battleground states. If we can pull off the impossible and win the Senate in 2018, Trump's judicial agenda is dead in its tracks.

Our success in blocking Trump's judges rests entirely on our ability to convince Democratic senators to hold firm in blanket opposition to any and all judicial appointments during his illegitimate presidency. So lobby them hard! And gear up to win the Senate in 2018.

28

FIGHT FOR EDUCATION

RECOMMENDED RESOURCES
American Federation of Teachers
National Education Association
NetworkforPublicEducation.org
ReclaimOurSchools.org

FUN FACT: ACCORDING to data crunched by statistician Nate Silver, Hillary Clinton outperformed President Barack Obama's electoral numbers in forty-eight of the fifty most educated counties in the country, and did so significantly, by an average margin of 8.5 points. Those counties ranged from diverse, like San Francisco and Fulton County, Georgia, to mostly white, like Chittenden County, Vermont. They included suburban and urban counties, and many counties in red states. The more educated the voting population, the more likely Clinton would post big gains.

Novel Ideas Books and Gifts

480 East Main Street
Decatur, IL 62523
(217) 429-1995
www.novelideasgifts.com

May 2, 2018
3:46 PM

Receipt gVN5	Cash
10 Resistance Handbook 44-0647	$12.99
Bargain Book Bargain	$1.00
Book - Used 5 Book 08-2223	$5.00
Book Club (20% off)	−$2.60

Subtotal	$16.39
Sales Tax	$1.52

Total	**$17.91**
Cash	$20.00
Change	$2.09

Return Policy: We will be glad to exchange
or issue store credit for new unopened
items. Sorry...no cash refunds.

Novel Ideas Books and Gifts

480 East Main Street	May 2, 2018
Decatur, IL 62523	3:46 PM
(217) 429 1995	
www.novelideasgifts.com	

Receipt QVNS	Cash

10	$12.99
Resistance Handbook 44-0647	
Bargain Book	$1.00
Bargain	
Book - Used	$5.00
S Book	
08-2223	
Book Club	–$2.60
(20% off)	

| Subtotal | $16.39 |
| Sales Tax | $1.52 |

Total	$17.91
Cash	$20.00
Change	$2.09

Return Policy: We will be glad to exchange
or issue store credit for new unopened
items. Sorry, no cash refunds

You know the flip side, right? In the fifty least educated counties, Clinton lost ground to Obama in forty-seven of them, for an average reduction of eleven points. "It appears as though educational levels are the critical factor in predicting shifts in the vote between 2012 and 2016," concluded Silver. In short, Republicans are losing educated voters and making gains with the undereducated.

Republicans, as a matter of course, target anything they consider an ideological threat. As an increasingly white, rural party, the GOP is trying to ban immigrants, who will probably turn into Democrats. It's the reason they try to disenfranchise black voters, who overwhelmingly vote Democratic. It's the reason they break labor unions, because they organize Democrats.

So yes, the reason Republicans attack education is because educated voters tend to vote for Democrats. "I've changed because of many factors, but I know that college and graduate school made a difference," wrote Salon writer Edwin Lyngar, a conservative-turned-liberal. "I met people unlike myself and was forced to defend sometimes ugly political positions. The Tea Party thrives on blue-collar 'common sense' that is composed of a combination of ignorance, superstition and fear. A literate and educated populace is an existential threat to the kind of thoughtless rage that has consumed the right over the past few years."

A LITERATE AND EDUCATED POPULACE IS AN EXISTENTIAL THREAT TO THE KIND OF THOUGHTLESS RAGE THAT HAS CONSUMED THE RIGHT OVER THE PAST FEW YEARS.

THE LIBERAL CONSPIRACY . . . AKA "THE ENLIGHTENMENT"

Convinced that education is some grand conspiracy to churn out liberals—after all, what's more liberal than science, logic, and facts?—conservatives have set out to destroy public education, from pre-K through college. During Trump's inaugural rant, he whined about our "education system flush with cash but which leaves our young and beautiful students deprived of all knowledge."

Trump immediately set out to turn his nonsense into reality by nominating billionaire supporter Betsy DeVos to be education secretary. DeVos, an anti-LGBTQ activist and funder of Christianist radicals, is also an avid proponent of the charter school boom that has cost untold billions. True to Republican form, those charter schools (which are a form of school privatization paid for with public funds) are also an abject failure: contrary to their proponents, they don't improve student performance over existing public schools.

And in addition to all that, DeVos was functionally illiterate when it came to matters of education. During her confirmation hearings, DeVos offered her support for guns in school "to protect from potential grizzlies," said supporting students with disabilities was "a matter that's best left to the states," and refused to commit to existing policies on the reporting of sexual assaults on college campuses. When asked by Senator Al Franken about the debate on test scores, DeVos was stunned into silence. She had no idea what Franken was talking about! "It surprises me that you don't know this issue," Franken sighed in response. "Ignorance apparently is bliss . . . even when you are about to be in charge of the education of America's youth."

So what can we do to fight back against Trump and the GOP's never-ending war on education?

1. **Support teachers.** Their jobs have been unfortunately politicized by frustrated conservatives. Many teachers use their own scarce resources to make up for funding shortfalls for basic school supplies. Support them with verbal encouragement, gifts, and support during union contract times, and publicly defend them when under attack.

2. **Control school boards.** The early conservative movement heavily targeted school board seats, both to influence what kids were learning and to build a bench for higher office. Let's take those boards back. Organize locally around those races. Recruit candidates or run yourself. And give those races the serious attention they deserve. They're in charge of our kids' education, after all.

3. **Protect kids from conservative policies.** DeVos supports "character development" in schools. And who wouldn't? Except those words are code for putting more police in schools and criminalizing school misbehavior. In fact, such tactics have created a new "school-to-prison pipeline" that exacerbates institutional disadvantages already facing poor children: black and LGBTQ children are the most likely to be disciplined under these "zero-tolerance" policies. (According to a GLSEN survey, 15 percent of LGBTQ children had been suspended, and 40 percent had received some sort of discipline.)

4. **Push school boards for more civics training.** Conservatives lose when children know how the nation's political system works; they can't afford an informed, engaged, and ready-to-vote population of young adults. Only 25 percent of children reach proficiency on the National Assessment of Educational Progress' Civics Assessment. White students, who benefit from systemic bias in school funding (among other advantages), are

up to *six* times more likely to pass than blacks or Latinos. So make sure your child's school has a proper civics curriculum, including the history of the civil rights movement and our Constitution. Then make sure your *state* helps fund such education.

5. **Fight for greater and more equitable school funding.** Public education is consistently shortchanged by state governments, especially in this era of Republican local dominance. Advocate and lobby for more funding, and don't be satisfied if your suburban school is doing fine. No student's education should be affected by where they live.

6. **Free college!** According to the College Board, the average tuition in 2017 is $33,480 for private schools and $9,650 for public schools. That doesn't include all associated fees and room and board. Multiply that times four years, and the pain is real. While students used to be able to pay for school with part-time jobs and some grants and loans, those days ended with the growing adoption of Republican-style tax cuts and concomitant austerity budgets. According to a study by the Education Trust, the best low-income students in eighth grade are less likely to go to college than the worst high-income students. We need a level playing field.

7. **Win elections.** Little of the above will happen with Republicans in charge.

A well-functioning education system that services *everyone* isn't just important for financial success and global competitiveness but also provides students with the experience that breaks through conservative bubbles. A well-rounded, educated, globally literate adult will be less susceptible to right-wing propaganda. Four or more years spent living, studying, and partying with people from all walks of life makes people less susceptible to racial animus, misogyny, and demagoguery.

Conservative dominance depends on enforced illiteracy. If you want to turn the progressive movement into a permanent enduring majority, education is the place to start.

29

PROTECT THE ENVIRONMENT

RECOMMENDED RESOURCES

350.org
EarthJustice.org
League of Conservation Voters
NextGenClimate.org
NRDC.org/Trump-Watch
SierraClub.org
SurfRider.org
Union of Concerned Scientists
WildernessSociety.org

DONALD TRUMP'S first one hundred days were devoid of any legislative accomplishments, while many of his top-priority agenda items—like the Muslim ban—were blocked by courts. His Mexican wall was a nonstarter in Congress, where Republicans who *live along the Mexican border* shot it down. It is difficult to *build* things, as the illegitimate, weak loser discovered. *Tearing stuff down*, on the other hand, is much easier.

When it comes to the environment, that's the GOP's specialty: its agenda on public lands, public health, and climate change is 100 percent death and destruction.

In the first one hundred days, Trump undermined America's commitment to a crucial international agreement on climate change; appointed an avowed climate-change denier to run the US Environmental Protection Agency; rolled back the Clean Power Plan, one of the Obama administration's signal achievements in reducing pollution; appointed the CEO of Exxon—Exxon!—as the nation's highest diplomat; changed the Bureau of Land Management's website to focus on coal extraction (with 250 million acres under its control—one-eighth of the entire nation—the BLM is the largest landowner in the United States); announced "reviews" of regulations protecting clean air and clean water; blocked regulation of a pesticide that's a known carcinogen; worked to expedite industry approval of toxic chemicals; erased all mention of climate change from government websites; erased mountains of public data on climate science; cut billions in funding for our national parks; cut earth science funding from NASA and the National Oceanic and Atmospheric Administration; approved the Dakota XL pipeline; began the process of rolling back higher automobile fuel efficiency standards; threatened to undermine California's leadership in clean energy and climate change; and summarily executed Smokey Bear.

Okay, he didn't really kill Smokey. But he did approve a rule that allows fake "hunters" to slaughter wolf pups and bears while they hibernate in their dens. In a sign of just how anti-conservation his administration is, even the *hunting community* attacked Trump over the threats to public lands and fish and wildlife habitat. Backcountry

Hunters and Anglers, for example, has decried the Republican's "war on public lands," expressed concern over Trump's attacks on public lands that "could harm fish and wildlife, reduce hunting and angling opportunities," and demanded "the new Administration must listen to the voices of American sportsmen who want more clean water, more fish and wildlife habitat, and new progress building on the successes of the past." Hunters killed a similar attempt to legalize bear baiting in Maine in 2014.

"I, and many staff, firmly believe that policies this Administration is advancing are contrary to what the majority of the American people, who pay our salaries, want EPA to accomplish, which are to ensure the air their children breathe is safe; the land they live, play, and hunt on to be free of toxic chemicals; and the water they drink, the lakes they swim in, and the rivers they fish in to be clean," wrote Michael Cox, a longtime veteran of the Environmental Protection Agency, in his resignation letter to EPA chief Scott Pruitt. "The message we are hearing is that this Administration is working to dismantle the EPA, and its staff, as quickly as possible."

Of course he is. Pruitt had been Oklahoma's attorney general, proving his antienvironmental bona fides by filing a series of legal challenges against the EPA, such as regulations limiting carbon emissions from electrical power plants and methane emissions from oil and gas extraction. In his LinkedIn page, Pruitt bragged about being "a leading advocate against the EPA's activist agenda." (For good measure, he also sued the Obama administration over immigration, the contraception mandate in the Affordable Care Act, and Wall Street reforms. He's the full Trumpian package.)

THE CLEAN ECONOMY IS HERE—AND EXXON IS PANICKING

During the Obama years, Pruitt, Trump, and the Republican Party had to watch helplessly as the clean technology industry blossomed and environmental conservation solidified its central role in supporting the economies of a growing majority of US states. As of today, our environmental regulations and rules protecting public lands are far more dominant in the economy than old, polluting industries like coal, oil, and natural gas. According to the Sierra Club, clean energy jobs outnumber fossil fuel jobs by more than 2.5 to 1; clean energy employs more Americans than fossil fuels in nearly every state. And according to the Outdoor Industry Association, there are 7.1 million Americans working in jobs related to the outdoors—nearly 100 times as many as work in the entire United States coal industry, at 76,000 workers.

ACCORDING TO THE SIERRA CLUB, CLEAN ENERGY JOBS OUTNUMBER FOSSIL FUEL JOBS BY MORE THAN 2.5 TO 1; CLEAN ENERGY EMPLOYS MORE AMERICANS THAN FOSSIL FUELS IN NEARLY EVERY STATE. AND THERE ARE 7.1 MILLION AMERICANS WORKING IN JOBS RELATED TO THE OUTDOORS—NEARLY 100 TIMES AS MANY AS WORK IN THE ENTIRE UNITED STATES COAL INDUSTRY, AT 76,000 WORKERS.

And what underpins these economic success stories? The very same regulations that Republicans consistently claim "kill jobs" and hinder economic growth: the Clean Air and Clean Water Acts, the National Environmental Policy Act, rules protecting public lands and parks, and incentives for investors to put money into solar and wind power, and electric vehicles.

Twenty years ago, it was easier to argue that environmental protection was a trade-off between jobs and polar bears. Today, our environmental regulations are leading drivers of technology innovation, giving rise to new industries, massive private-sector investments, job creation, and, yes, reduced pollution, improved public health, and (hopefully) happier bears.

The Trump administration is really the swan song of a dying way of life—digging up dead plants and rocks and burning them to run our cars and light our homes. As the largest industry on earth, fossil fuels won't go down without a fight. Unless we resist the Republican agenda, a great deal of damage will take place over the next four years. Here are some ways to contribute:

1. **Join environmental organizations at the national and local levels.** Organizations like the Sierra Club, Natural Resource Defense Council, National Wildlife Federation, BlueGreen Alliance, Environmental Defense Fund, and 350.org keep tabs on federal regulations, promote the clean economy, and have teams of lawyers at the ready to defend our bedrock public health and environmental protections. They'll alert you to important votes and regulatory proceedings, and keep you abreast of the latest developments—both the good news about clean energy and the threats of Pruitt's troglodyte agenda.

2. **Support biking, mass transit, and smart urban policy.** Perhaps the biggest lift in protecting the environment, for all of us, is learning to get out of our cars and using less polluting means of transport. It's not an option for everyone, but if you can, walk, ride a bike, or take the bus or train; if your community doesn't have these amenities, figure out who in your city is supporting transit issues and join them! Most major cities have bicycle coalitions and advocacy organizations that support infrastructure

for walking and transit. City politics around transit and biking are a mess in most places; jump in! You can have a huge impact by just showing up at a city council, transit board, or planning commission meeting and raising your voice. Chances are you'll find like-minded citizens in the chambers with you.

3. **Join the YIMBYs!** They're relatively new on the scene, but the "Yes in My Backyard" movement is taking on one of the toughest environmental battles we face in the United States: the need to slow the growth of the suburbs and provide more housing—for people of all income levels—in and around our urban cores, close to transit, shopping, and places of employment. This also supports less driving. Cars are the leading cause of climate pollution in the United States, so until we all have renewable fuel-powered all-electric vehicles, the best thing to do is reduce demand for cars. Along the way, we'll also have more affordable housing for our middle-income workers like teachers and firefighters, a win-win!

4. **Monitor what's happening with your Public Utility Commission.** This obscure political agency is actually one of the most powerful environmental regulators in the US, and there's one in every state. Commissioners answer to governors (or, in a few cases, the voters), so it's an area where you can have a great deal of influence and impact. PUCs control the flow of water and energy in your state—electricity from power plants, wind farms, and hydro facilities, plus natural gas pipelines for heating and cooking. A host of specialized energy advocacy groups track PUC activities and lobby for more energy efficiency and renewable energy. You can find information about your state's programs through DSIRE, or join Vote Solar, Advanced Energy Economy, the American Wind Energy Association, or the American Council for an Energy-Efficient Economy.

5. **Shop smart and politicize your consumerism.** A growing number of companies are finding that they can no longer get away with "greenwashing" and must certify that their products are green and sustainably sourced, and that they treat workers fairly regardless of where they manufacture. Business for Social Responsibility tracks many of these companies, along with the various certifications; there are also groups like the Sustainable Apparel Coalition and CDP, which has a growing list of firms working to reduce their climate pollution. Organizations like Greenpeace do amazing work tracking down the worst corporate environmental offenders and holding their feet to the fire; support them. If you don't always have time to closely monitor your shopping, do the basics: bring your own bags to reduce plastic waste, compost your food scraps, reduce purchases of items that come with excessive packaging, and avoid processed foods. (This last step will also improve your diet.)

6. **Get outside! Enjoy your parks and public lands.** There's nothing better for the soul than spending time outside in nature; as we discussed earlier, it's important that members of the Resistance take time to rejuvenate and refresh. Do it in your local city or state park, or visit one of our beautiful national parks. Outdoor visits aren't just good for your mind and body; by showing up and using these lands for rest, relaxation, and recreation, you'll show land managers that people really care about their proper stewardship. It's much harder to bulldoze a place when it's full of hikers and picnickers.

7. **Volunteer for cleanups, restoration projects, and other conservation activities.** Whether it's a river cleanup, a beach cleanup, trail maintenance, or a fish count, you probably live within a few miles of some form of opportunity to conserve

the nature in your backyard. The Nature Conservancy organizes activities around the country (and around the world), and there are local orgs that can also use your help.

8. **Get to know some hunters and/or fishermen.** This is a tough one for many of us on the left, but it turns out that some of the most strident environmentalists in the United States carry guns and fishing poles. The reason? There's no game to hunt when the habitat has been destroyed, and fish don't swim in polluted rivers. Sportsmen may not always share our political perspectives, but they are natural allies in our fight to protect our shared heritage. And who knows, maybe they'll share a rainbow trout or elk steak with you. Learn more about the sportsmen's conservation movement through Trout Unlimited, the Teddy Roosevelt Conservation Partnership, and Sportsmen for Responsible Energy Development.

9. **Keep track of your state's Department of Environmental Quality.** As much as we focus on federal environmental protections, the truth is that states implement these laws, and their performance is largely determined by state politics. For example, Texas and California both have large oil industries, but which state do you think is cracking down harder on air pollution? DEQs typically answer to governors, and state advocacy groups will keep track of the important stuff.

The battle to stem and even reverse climate change will be long and hard but particularly fraught over the next four years. By employing both political actions and personal behavior changes, we can go a long way in slowing Trump's efforts to turn America into one big polluted mine pit.

30

PROTECT OUR SOCIAL SAFETY NET

RECOMMENDED RESOURCES

EnrollAmerica.org
FamiliesUSA.org
SocialSecurityWorks.org

REPUBLICANS *REALLY* HATE Social Security. And they hate Medicare and Medicaid. And they hate Obamacare, formally known as the Affordable Care Act. In short, they hate anything that might involve the government's helping anyone for fear it might lead to "government dependency." Heaven forbid we give people a reason to appreciate and support the role of government in improving their lives!

"Never in the history of the world has any measure been brought here so insidiously designed as to prevent business recovery, to enslave workers and to prevent any possibility of the employers providing work for the people," said Representative John Taber in the 1935 debate over the creation of Social Security. Another Republican, Representative Daniel Reed, lamented that "the lash of the dictator will be felt and 25 million free American citizens will for the first time submit themselves to a fingerprint test." And for good measure, Representative James W. Wadsworth warned that Social Security would create a government "so vast, so powerful as to threaten the integrity of our institutions and to pull the pillars of the temple down upon the heads of our descendants."

Then a funny thing happened. Or rather . . . none of the things they warned of happened. But our seniors no longer died in squalid poorhouses, and our most destitute citizens had somewhere to turn when they were injured or sick or otherwise needed assistance.

A RATION OF BEER SOUNDS NICE, ACTUALLY

Then, in the sixties, as the debate over Medicare raged, conservative hero Ronald Reagan saw only decimation and ruin: "If Medicare passes into law, the consequences will be dire beyond imagining. One of these days you and I are going to spend our sunset years telling our children, and our children's children, what it once was like in America when men were free." Barry Goldwater, the father of American conservatism, was just as hyperbolic: "Having given our pensioners their medical care in kind, why not food baskets, why not public housing accommodations, why not vacation resorts, why not a ration of cigarettes for those who smoke and of beer for those who drink?"

And then *another* funny thing happened: Despite their dire predictions, Americans *liked* that helping hand! They didn't mind big government designed to help the people, rather than enable corporations to pillage the economy for the benefit of a few. But wait, it gets weirder: The economy grew! We added jobs! And rich people were . . . still rich!

Republicans were left to stew in anger, increasingly frustrated that their core ideology had been repeatedly proven false, and *apoplectic* that their efforts to undermine those entitlements always came up short. But it's no wonder that the GOP can never deliver on its promises of small government. Its base is old white people. Who are the biggest beneficiaries of these programs? Yup. Old white people.

Well, now you can add Obamacare to the list of Republican frustrations. Except that unlike Social Security and Medicare, the health insurance program doesn't target the elderly (they're already covered by Medicare), it doesn't have built-in incumbency, and it remains a highly charged partisan topic. Which is why after nearly one hundred votes to dismantle the program during the Obama years, it seemed like the program was doomed when they took full control of all three branches of government in January 2017.

But once again, Republicans were stymied by one simple fact: people like government help! People who instinctively disapproved of Obamacare because they were Republican suddenly decided to like the program because it benefited them. According to the Kaiser Family Foundation tracking poll of Obamacare's popularity, the program had a 45–43 unfavorable rating November 2016. By March 2017, as Republicans pushed their first failed repeal attempt, that number was 49–44 *favorable*.

But Republicans have all of these programs in the cross hairs and will continue to work to undermine them. So what can the Resistance do?

1. **Call, call, call!** Despite having congressional majorities, it took Republicans three tries to get their Obamacare repeal bill

through the House, and they were so damaged politically from the effort that Senate Republicans immediately announced that effort dead on arrival. The bill came two votes from failing with moderate and swing-district Republicans scared into opposition by the fierce public backlash. Your calls worked! So whenever these repeal or destroy efforts come up, go back to that trusty phone and dial away.

2. **Town halls work.** Yes, this is a rehash of other sections of the book, but it bears reinforcing—elected officials react in large part according to their face-to-face interactions with constituents.

3. **Elect Democrats.** There was a time when "serious" Democrats would talk about scaling back entitlement programs. Those were horrible Democrats, guided by horrible organizations like the Democratic Leadership Council and Third Way. Most of that talk is dead, and Democrats, led by Senator Elizabeth Warren, are now advocating *expanding* those programs. That was even part of Hillary Clinton's platform in 2016. Imagine that, trying to win elections by giving people more of the popular stuff! So yes, elect more Democrats, but especially those who promise to expand entitlement programs.

4. **Join groups focused on these topics.** Social Security Works, Enroll America, *Daily Kos*, and other groups all make defending these programs a priority. Make sure you are on their mailing lists so you are alerted when action is necessary.

5. **Help people sign up for Obamacare.** Given their difficulties in eliminating Obamacare legislatively, Trump will try to destroy it administratively. Among the tools at his disposal is cutting all outreach and advertising. If fewer people sign up, the program won't have the critical mass of enrollees and could collapse. So

be aware of the open enrollment period and make sure that everyone around you who isn't insured signs up.

Entitlements are popular, yet for too long, Democrats were afraid to enthusiastically champion them. Democrats were slow to rally around Obamacare, and they've only recently emerged from a dark period where they wanted to "save" Social Security and Medicare by gutting those programs. But our party, whatever its lingering problems, has come a long way on that issue, and it's our job to continue delivering that message.

Fight to defend and expand Social Security, Medicare, Medicaid, and Obamacare, not just because it's the right thing, but because it's also the smartest thing, politically.

31

PROTECT WORKERS' RIGHTS

RECOMMENDED RESOURCES

American Federation of State, County and Municipal Employees
Fightfor15.org
Service Employees International Union
WorkingAmerica.org

THE 2010 REPUBLICAN wave was a wholesale disaster for organized labor. With unified control of state government in key states, Republicans set about to dismantle unions in bedrock labor strongholds like Michigan and Pennsylvania. In Wisconsin, birthplace of the AFSCME, the large union representing government workers, Republican governor Scott Walker began his governorship by crushing those very same public employee unions. He signed "right-to-work legislation" that decimated private-sector unions, then removed all government requirements for union labor for taxpayer-funded programs.

In one fell swoop, Walker didn't just hand corporations a huge victory; he destroyed one of the Democratic Party's most stalwart allies and ground-game organizers.

It's no accident or coincidence that Donald Trump's 2016 victory was delivered by Michigan, Pennsylvania, and Wisconsin. And yes, voter disenfranchisement was one part of the puzzle, but killing organized labor was the other.

A FAIR DAY'S WORK FOR A FAIR DAY'S PAY

It certainly pays to be unionized, literally. According to the Bureau of Labor Statistics, union households earn, on average, $400 more than nonunion households per month. That's nearly $5,000 more per year. Over a lifetime of work, those union households earn over half a million dollars more than their nonorganized counterparts—wealth that Republicans think should stay in the hands of the moneyed elite.

So it was certainly ironic when, in 2016, Hillary Clinton won the union vote by just eight points, the smallest margin since the Walter Mondale debacle in 1984. President Barack Obama won those households by eighteen points in 2012. In Michigan, Clinton won union households by only thirteen points. Obama had won them by thirty-three in 2012. For Clinton, this was a double whammy—decimated unions weren't able to provide the ground operation from past cycles, while blue-collar white union workers were far more likely to support the Republican nominee than in previous cycles.

While popular-vote loser Donald Trump made deep inroads into these predominantly white working-class union households, once elected he wasted no time in stabbing them in the back. His first pick for labor secretary was Andy Puzder, a fast-food mogul who included Hardee's and Carl's Jr. in his portfolio. "You've made your fortune by squeezing the very workers you'd be charged with protecting as Labor Secretary out of wages and benefits," wrote Senator Elizabeth Warren in a letter to him, referring to the 108 Labor Department investigations into his businesses, 60 percent of which found evidence of wrongdoing. He was an outspoken opponent of a higher minimum wage, alleging against all empirical evidence that higher wages cost jobs.

Puzder's nomination collapsed because of allegations of spousal abuse, among other things. But Trump's nomination, and the Senate's confirmation, of Neil Gorsuch elevated a similarly strident antilabor voice to the Supreme Court. "In one case, he voted to overturn a fine issued by the Department of Labor against a company whose negligence caused an employee's death on the job," wrote Ron Bieber, head of the Michigan AFL-CIO. "In another case, Gorsuch sided with a health services company that improperly cut the wages of their employees, and was ordered to issue back payments."

Nothing shines a brighter spotlight on the Trump family's disdain for workers than one simple Donald Jr. tweet from June 22, 2012: "At dinner w our greenskeeper who missed his sister's wedding 2 work (luv loyalty 2 us) No big deal hopefully she'll have another someday;)." What kind of monster doesn't give his staff time off to attending their sibling's wedding? The Trump kind of monster.

ORGANIZED LABOR LITERALLY INVENTED THE WEEKEND.

So how do Resisters show their support for workers and the labor movement?

1. **Fight for a $15 minimum wage.** Everyone working should be able to earn a living wage—enough to afford rent, food, health care, daycare for their kids, transportation, and education expenses. Fifteen dollars an hour ends up being about $31,000 per year; while that's still not enough in many regions, states should look at their own minimum wages and other complementary policies. It's more than double the current federal minimum wage at $7.25. Future minimum-wage hikes should be automatic and pegged to inflation.

2. **Support labor laws.** Organized labor helps reset the balance of power between workers and management, with a corresponding transference of wealth to those putting in the work. Support laws like "card check" that make it easier for workers to unionize.

3. **Support organizing efforts.** Join in boycotts and other labor efforts to organize and improve the lives of their members.

4. **Support prolabor candidates for office at all levels.** The bulk of labor law is established at the state level. Be mindful of labor endorsements and support candidates who support workers.

The balance of power is tilted against the working class. Organized labor has been critical over our nation's history in addressing that imbalance, pioneering worker protections that apply to *all* workers. Organized labor literally invented the weekend! They also ended child labor, pioneered employer-provided health care, and helped create government-mandated family and medical leave. *And*, on top of all that, they work hard to get voters to the polls. A strong labor movement is good for workers and good for democracy. Fight for the right of workers to organize and earn a living wage.

BUILD ELECTORAL INFRASTRUCTURE

3 2

REGISTER PEOPLE TO VOTE

RECOMMENDED RESOURCES

Election Assistance Commission
ProjectVote.org
RocktheVote.com
Vote411.org
Women's Voices Women Vote

WE'VE LOOKED AT the stats already: Hillary Clinton won the election by around three million votes, the forty-three Democrats in the Senate minority have collectively received twenty-three million more votes than the fifty-two Republicans in the supposed majority, and in most election cycles this past decade, Democratic House candidates have received more votes than the Republicans. Our system is rigged in a way that undermines our nation's democratic promise, and work needs to be done to fix that.

However, the reality is that none of the above should matter. There are more of *us* than there are of *them*. Yet we must heighten our focus on elections because our people, in huge numbers, *do not vote*.

In the 2016 presidential election, nearly 42 percent of eligible voters did not cast a ballot. In real numbers, that's—hold on to your seat!—*ninety-seven million voters*. While a certain quarter of the progressive coalition argues over winning back working-class whites, we have NINETY-SEVEN MILLION potential voters sitting on the sidelines!

These nonvoters are predominantly members of core Democratic constituencies, young and/or from communities of color. In Wayne County, home of Detroit, 75,000 Motown Obama voters skipped voting for Hillary Clinton. Donald Trump won the state by less than 12,000 votes, but it shouldn't even have been *that* close, because while there are 1.349 million residents of voting age in Wayne County, just 758,000 turned out to vote. Wayne County favored Clinton over Trump 66–30; all those dormant voters could've put Michigan safely away by several hundred thousand votes. It's the same story in Wisconsin and Pennsylvania.

Let's look at Texas, a red state fast trending purple. Trump won the state by 807,000 votes. Texas Latinos opted for Clinton by a margin of 61–34, according to exit polls. Those polls also show that 24 percent of voters in the state were Latino—about 2.06 million voters. However, according to data from Pew Research, there are 4.82 million Latinos eligible to vote in the state, which means over 2.8 million sat on the sidelines. Had they voted at the same rate as Latinos who *did* vote, it would've added an extra 1.1 million votes to Clinton's tally, and—bam!—just like that, *Texas would be blue*. And comfortably so, without even including young white voters, African-Americans, and single women voters, all of which similarly underperform. It hurts to think about, doesn't it?

THAT'S RIGHT, THE WOMEN ARE . . . NOT VOTING AS MUCH AS THEY COULD

We've discussed how single women are a critical Democratic constituency. Yet in 2014 (the latest data available at this point), 22.4 million single women didn't vote, while another 14.2 million were registered to vote and sat out the midterms. End result, of 56.8 million eligible voters, just 20.2 million cast ballots, and Republicans laughed all the way to the bank, winning more state legislatures and congressional seats. If we motivated these women to vote, none of these elections would be close; traditional red states would become battlegrounds, not just at the presidential level but down the ballot.

It's therefore critical that we do everything we can to mobilize these potential voters, get them registered, and then G-O-T-V. So if you're ever at a loss for something to do to support the Resistance, go out and sign people up. With a ninety-seven-million-potential-voter backlog, we won't run out of people to register for a long time.

1. **Register your immediate social circle.** Make sure everyone in your immediate social circle, such as friends, family, and coworkers, is registered to vote. The biggest political influencers will always be people they know. If everyone in the Resistance registered five nonvoting acquaintances, we'd be in much better shape. And we're willing to bet everyone knows five people who don't vote.

2. **Get acquainted with your local voter registration rules.** Some

states have age requirements for registration gatherers. Look at registration deadlines, residency requirements, and other guidelines. Many states try to make the process harder as a way to disenfranchise voters. If you are in one of those states, it sucks, but you'll just have to work harder and smarter. If your state requires voter ID, you may have to help people get those, too.

3. **Get your local activism group to register voters.** We are fighting a lot of battles, on a lot of fronts. But during any quiet period, get your group to register voters!

4. **Join an established voter-registering group.** The League of Women Voters has been registering voters for decades.

5. **Get your house of worship to register voters.** Conservatives use their churches to further their political aims. Progressive-minded houses of worship should work to empower their congregations and communities by encouraging not just their own voting participation but that of the broader community in their neighborhood.

6. **Go to high-traffic areas to prospect for nonvoters.** Set up registration tables in campuses, malls, theaters, and other high-traffic areas. Resist the urge to prospect the local Whole Foods; that crowd is already likely highly engaged. Sure, it's comfortable, but you're trying to get our low-performing demographics engaged, and that requires going to where people of color, the economically disadvantaged, and young adults live and congregate.

Republicans do a great job turning out their voters. We do not. The political spoils go to those who show up. The challenge might be daunting—*ninety-seven million unregistered voters!*—but there are millions of us in the Resistance. Together, working diligently, we can make it virtually impossible for Republicans to win elections.

33

HELP THE CENSUS COUNT EVERYONE

RECOMMENDED RESOURCES

Census.gov
CivilRights.org

IN 2010, CANADA'S then–prime minister, conservative Stephen Harper, decided to make the long version of his country's census form optional. Response rates plummeted from 93.5 percent the previous census to 68.6 percent. Nonrespondents disproportionately included poor, immigrant, aboriginal, and other marginalized communities.

Cities suddenly had a dearth of the information they needed to make decisions, such as how to plan public health campaigns. There were open questions as to the actual population of Canada. And since legislative seats and government resources are distributed based on population, undercounting urban centers meant the loss of both proportional representation and federal funding. As one economist put it, half-jokingly, "Because of the move to the voluntary [census survey], Canada is a richer, whiter, more educated country now!"

That's certainly the Republican Party's dream, isn't it? What if federal dollars could be deployed in a way that screwed the same marginalized communities that voted against Trump and the GOP? What if Republicans could perpetuate the system of inequity, poverty, and marginalization that depresses voter participation? Heck, what if conservatives could pretend that the nation's demographic trends weren't as dire for their future prospects? There would be less political pressure to reform their party to be more inclusive and tolerant, and they could continue on their path to white nationalism without worrying about the electoral consequences.

BE LIKE CANADA—THE *NEW* CANADA

One of the first acts of newly elected liberal Canadian prime minister Justin Trudeau was to reinstate the mandatory full-length census, but here in the United States, we may be headed in the opposite direction. The census in this country doesn't just determine how much funding cities and states receive from the federal government, it also determines the boundaries of congressional and state legislative districts. Undercounting marginalized communities directly disenfranchises them and perpetuates the cycle of disempowerment.

Trump's war on immigrants, for example, will almost assuredly dampen response rates in those communities. "If you imagine that the federal government is asking for personal information and you feel that the federal government is hostile and that if you were to answer this, perhaps they would use this against you," Terry Ao Minnis, director of the census and voting programs at Asian Americans Advancing Justice, told *Politico*. "That, of course, will make people less inclined to participate." While the traditional census doesn't ask about immigration status, Republicans are insisting that the new one do so. Immigrants, including legal ones, could rightly wonder why a government that's openly hostile to their presence is collecting that information.

In any case, Trump is already trying to underfund the census. While the agency has requested a $290 million increase to ramp up the hiring it needs to fulfill its mission—it needs hundreds of thousands of people to gather the data—Republicans appear set to offer only $100 million. This is the flip side of the GOP's legendary voter-suppression tactics. They make it harder for our people to be heard and counted, and make it easier for Republicans to win elections.

The shenanigans extend to the census' American Community Survey, which gathers additional data during in-between census years. Republicans have already clamped down on data collection efforts at the Environmental Protection Agency and the US Department of Agriculture. Bills are circulating that would block the production and distribution of data about racial segregation. And as mentioned earlier, Republicans have already stripped out a question about sexual orientation and gender identity from the census, afraid to get an accurate count of our nation's LGBTQ population.

Republicans don't want us counted. They don't want data that exposes institutional bias and inequality. We must fight back.

1. **Educate.** Before the actual census arrives, spread the word about its importance. Impress on people what happens with census data and why Republicans would want to use it to disenfranchise our communities. A flawed census reinforces the

existing broken system. We need people *angry* and motivated to fill out the census form when it arrives.

2. **Engage corporate allies.** Corporations rely on census data to make all manner of decisions. It is the foundation of most market research. It is in their interests to have an accurate census. At least in this instance, we can leverage their outsize influence on the political process to our benefit.

3. **Engage your local organizing group.** Educate local activists about the importance of the census and GOP efforts to disenfranchise and disempower communities, and come up with a plan to spread the word (early in the process) and participate (when 2020 rolls around).

4. **Demand full census funding.** House Republicans do not have a functional majority in Congress with a rabid right-wing faction allergic to compromise on government funding issues. That gives Democrats leverage in budget negotiations. Write and call your federal legislators (regardless of party) demanding full funding of the Census Bureau.

As esoteric and far away as the Census may seem, Republicans are already working to undermine the nation's head count, further cementing their structural, political, and economic advantages. Skew the census in the direction of the GOP's base, and it's not hard to see who ultimately benefits. It is our job, in the Resistance, to thwart those efforts.

34

DONATE TO CAMPAIGNS

RECOMMENDED RESOURCES

ActBlue.com
MovementVote.org
TogetherList.com

ELECTIONS RUN ON money, and that's not an objectively "bad" thing. Campaign staff need salaries; they also need offices and equipment, design and advertising budgets, database infrastructure, polling, direct mail, and all the other trappings of a modern political campaign.

Liberals, being liberals, have an aversion to money, and particularly the distortive effects it can have on our politics. That's only natural, since we've seen time and again how special-interest dollars—especially, but not exclusively, from self-interested billionaires—can make a mockery of our democratic ideals. The distorting influence of money ensures that, rather than have a one-person, one-vote system, those with the most financial resources have a disproportionate say in our democracy.

Yet we can't escape the reality that campaigns still need money. We're getting much better at raising it; slowly but surely, small donors are showing the power of collective contributions to progressive candidates: Bernie Sanders raised $228 million during the 2016 cycle, nearly 60 percent of it from small donors (under $200). In contrast, just 19 percent of Hillary Clinton's donations came from small donors. For the Republican National Committee, it was less than 5 percent.

In April 2017, in a House special election in the Atlanta suburbs, Democratic candidate Jon Ossoff raised over $9 million from 195,000 mostly small-dollar donors, averaging $42.50 per individual. It was a record-setting haul for a House candidate, fueled by grassroots Democrats wanting to send Donald Trump a message.

IN OUR DEMOCRACY, MONEY IS (STILL) SPEECH

It would be ludicrous to argue that Bernie Sanders was "bought and paid for" by his army of supporters, or that Ossoff has been corrupted by the flow of small-dollar money into *his* campaign. In fact, this might be some of the purest expression of democracy—people supporting candidates because they *believe* in the individual and that person's agenda, rather than how that politician can personally enrich them.

Let's do some math. If all five million people who participated in the Women's March donated $50, on average, to House candidates, that would equal *$250 million*. For context, the 907 Democrats who ran for the House in 2016 raised a *total* of $275 million (matched almost to the dollar by House Republican candidates). That kind of money would be politically transformational, helping dramatically expand the map and diluting the effect of special-interest money on our candidates.

IT WOULD BE LUDICROUS TO ARGUE THAT BERNIE SANDERS WAS "BOUGHT AND PAID FOR" BY HIS ARMY OF SUPPORTERS, OR THAT OSSOFF HAS BEEN CORRUPTED BY THE FLOW OF SMALL-DOLLAR MONEY INTO HIS CAMPAIGN.

Given the tilt of the Supreme Court (which has ruled more than once that money is a form of speech, starting with *Buckley v. Valeo* in 1976), it's not clear that there's a pathway to get all money out of politics; it's not even clear that that would be desirable. One way or another, elected officials and their staff need to eat; travel around their districts, states, and the nation; and convince voters to vote for them.

But there are many ways we can use our home-field advantage to leverage the power of small donations and turn them into something big.

1. **Start local.** Starting at the local level, work to support and build a strong bench of elected progressives. Not only is local policy critical, but local elected officials are the farm team that become the representatives, senators, and presidents of tomorrow.

2. **Give to people who inspire you.** Let the party committees worry about putting money where "we have the best chance to win." You don't have to give to the party. Instead, look for candidates who inspire you and reward them with your money. Running for office is hard, thankless work. It's even harder if you're running in hostile territory. *Those* are our greatest heroes. Even a few bucks goes a long way, not just to help fund their campaigns, but to validate their sacrifice and hard work.

3. **Be okay with losing.** Building a long-term movement, one based on a fifty-state strategy, means we'll often contest seats with little chance of winning. The *Daily Kos* community sent

nearly $200,000 to a special-election Democratic candidate in a deep-red Wichita-area district in Kansas. People donated knowing full well victory would be tough, but it was all worth it when we lost by seven points in a district Trump had won by twenty-seven. When we're in a deep hole, we claw back incrementally. And in some of these districts, a little money goes a long way.

4. **Encourage people around you to donate.** You are the biggest political influencer in your circle. Amplify your donations by getting people around you to follow suit. Host a fundraiser. Send people to your ActBlue page.

Finally, get comfortable with the role of money in politics. Remember, the problem isn't the cash itself but the *source* of it. The more grassroots Democrats help fund our candidates, the less beholden they will be to nefarious special interests. And the less beholden to special interests they are, the more responsive they can be to their constituents. And the more responsive they are to constituents?

Well, that's what victory looks like. Let's make it happen.

35

TALK TO PEOPLE

RECOMMENDED RESOURCES
ActionGroups.net
KnockEveryDoor.org
Member Policy Advocacy & Campaign Teams

THE SINGLE MOST effective way to turn out voters, bar none, is with face-to-face interactions. A 1998 study by Alan Gerber and Don Green found that door knockers—or what we call "canvassers"—boosted voter turnout by 20 percent. Another study by David Broockman and Joshua Kalla found that face-to-face canvassing interactions dramatically reduced anti-transgender prejudice. "We found that a single, approximately 10-minute conversation with a stranger produced large reductions in prejudice that persisted for at least the three months studied to date, were resistant to counterargument and affected political attitudes," said Broockman. In fact, that *ten-minute* conversation decreased prejudice by the same amount that the entire LGBTQ had managed *in over a decade of advocacy work.*

The key ingredient: trust. Unless you've met before in person, nobody really knows each other online. But interact with someone and have a shared experience with them, and you've laid the groundwork for a trusting relationship.

EYES ON THE PRIZE: IN-PERSON CONTACT BUILDS TRUST

Talking to people face-to-face is important! Conservatives know this and have thoroughly politicized their church network to facilitate that in-person indoctrination. Religious conservatives didn't care that Trump was morally odious, because trusted leaders in their in-person social circle had delivered clear instructions: the only thing that mattered in the election was the Supreme Court seat that the GOP stole from Obama.

Imagine if the Left had the same sort of trust networks to get *Citizens United*–hating liberals to focus with laser-like precision on the court, rather than whip themselves into a frenzy online over Hillary Clinton's "neoliberalism." Conservatives used their in-person networks to keep their eye on the ball, while we got bogged down in internecine fighting online.

And those divisions on the Left might have even been stoked by Russian saboteurs! No one knows who anyone is online, and we know the Kremlin has a "troll army" whose job is to flood the Internet with propaganda in support of President Vladimir Putin's agenda. (And electing Trump was certainly part of his agenda.) No Russian trolls will knock on our door.

The power of in-person indoctrination is also why conservatives are working so hard to de-politicize college campuses; young people talking to each other about tolerance, equality, and sustainability presents an existential long-term threat to their ideology. The more we foster a culture of open political dialogue with people around us, the stronger our ability to move politics in our direction.

But here's the irony: liberals are actually not afraid to talk about *issues*. There's a reason we do so well winning the culture wars, whether it's marriage equality, access to contraception, or accepting Irish Catholics as "real" Americans. It's the reason Democrats have majority support on the issues of education, the environment, the economy, immigration, Trump's stupid wall, the Muslim ban, and a woman's right to choose. And yet . . . we keep losing elections. It's not enough to just talk about issues. We must do more.

1. **Talk elections.** There is a strain of liberal that considers elections and the political process icky. People yell at each other and disagree and it's all very upsetting! Much better to stick to the intellectual realm of issues, where facts and figures and logic can win the day! Except that without holding electoral power, none of our issues will get the treatment they deserve. You cannot have one without the other. So sure, keep talking issues, but also tie those issues to the importance of electoral participation.

2. **Politicize your immediate social circle.** If you're reading this book, you are probably the most politically engaged person in your social circle. (Marketers would call you an "influencer.") So make sure to talk to your friends, family, and coworkers about the importance of engaging electorally. Find out their favorite issues, and use those as gateways into conversations about electoral participation. Remind them that ninety-seven million voting-eligible people did not participate in the 2016 elections giving Republicans full control. If you're talking to a nonvoter,

work at getting them to register and vote. If you're talking to a voter, work on getting them to be an activist.

3. **Politicize your casual conversations.** It has been amazing seeing the dramatic politicization of even casual encounters in the wake of the 2016 elections. We've had baggers at the checkout line at a grocery store ask about the latest Trump craziness. The drop-off line at school is nothing but politics. Even the sidelines at our children's sports contests. So politicize small talk, dropping seeds into people's minds that could grow into better education and political engagement.

4. **Canvass!** Go outside your immediate circle and talk to people in their homes. The efficacy of canvassing is undeniable. The Broockman and Kalla study referenced above found that canvassing reduced anti-transgender bigotry regardless of whether the person was Republican, Democrat, or independent, whether they were white, Latino, or African-American, and whether they were women or men. Those in-person conversations were able to bust through ideological bubbles in a way that media and online interactions never can.

5. **Have real conversations.** Don't sound like a TV commercial. Scripted canvassing, where volunteers rush through to cram as much information as they can into a voter's mind, is as useful as TV ads. In other words, not useful at all. To be persuasive, the exchanges have to be authentic.

None of this should be surprising. We are, by nature, social animals. Talk to people in your circle and canvass outside it, and don't be shy about talking about how elections impact the issues people care about. Those conversations will be the most effective tool we have in convincing the legions of nonvoting liberals to help take back control of our democracy.

36

VOLUNTEER ON A CAMPAIGN

RECOMMENDED RESOURCES

CodeforDemocracy.io
RagTag.org
SisterDistrict.com
TechforCampaigns.org
VisibleResistance.org
Young Democrats of America

CAMPAIGNS MAY SPEND big money on staff, but their lifeblood is volunteers. It is volunteers who fill up the phone banks, reaching out to potential voters. It is volunteers who do the bulk of the canvassing, talking to potential voters door-to-door. It is volunteers who lick stamps and stuff envelopes, do data entry, act as guides and crowd control at campaign events, represent the campaign during local parades, and staff booths at county fairs. Volunteers don't just provide people power for the campaign's operations, they also inspire candidates, giving them much-needed validation that can sustain them throughout a grueling campaign season.

If you want better elected officials in your city, county, state, and Washington, DC, there are few better ways to make that happen than to directly engage as a volunteer.

1. **Focus locally . . .** Yes, there are probably swing districts and sexy campaigns elsewhere, but we won't build the local, fifty-state party infrastructure we need unless activists take care of their backyard first. That doesn't mean you ignore stuff outside of your home base, but give your local progressive candidates at least some of your time and energy. And it doesn't matter where you live; no matter how blue or red, there is *always* someone who could use your help.

2. **. . . Then nationally.** Every cycle, there are key battleground races that get all the attention, and then there are others that are more peripheral. *Daily Kos* generally cedes the big expensive battleground districts to the party and focuses on expanding the playing field by sending resources to second- and third-tier contests. If successful, those races graduate to top-tier status, and the site has successfully helped broaden the map. You can decide for yourself—focus on the races that get all the attention, or help broaden the map by looking at less heavily contested races. *Daily Kos* will track races by tiers, while organizations like Sister District will match up volunteers with competitive contests elsewhere in the country.

3. **Show up.** Sign up to volunteer for a campaign, giving them

an idea of what tasks you can handle. There's canvassing, phone-banking, delivering yard signs, data entry, clerical work, leafleting, driving the candidate, waving signs at busy intersections, and even cleaning up the office. No task is too small! They must all get done. And for some of these, you don't even need to wait for the campaign to call you back! Print out some flyers and go hand them out.

4. **Host a fundraiser or meet-and-greet.** Campaigns are always looking for locations to host events. If you have the space in your home or office, offer to host.

5. **Donate supplies.** Every campaign needs printer paper, toner cartridges, pens, trash bags, coffee supplies, etc. Collect stuff around your house and office, then get your friends and coworkers to chip in. Track everything, by person, so it can be properly reported on campaign finance forms.

6. **Bring food.** Pizza is great, but campaigning doesn't lend itself to healthy eating. So anything more . . . *sophisticated* is hugely appreciated. Also, don't forget the vegetarians and vegans among us when helping out!

7. **Talk up your campaign to everyone around you.** Heck, wear a campaign T-shirt if you can get one. Remember that most people are unaware of down-ballot races, so this is your big opportunity to educate potential voters about who is running and why they should care.

8. **Do Election Day outreach.** Work polling locations asking people to vote for your candidate. Don't engage people who want to argue; they're trying to waste your time so you can't reach other reachable voters. Drive voters to the polls. Wave signs at busy intersections.

9. **Special skills? Offer them!** If you are a lawyer, offer to help

with campaign law matters or election protection on Election Day. If you are an accountant, volunteer those skills. Are you tech savvy or a developer? Everyone needs help with technology. Are you an organizational genius? Volunteer to organize volunteers! Most small, under-resourced campaigns will have trouble deploying even a small number of volunteers.

The Democratic Party is in its current predicament, in large part, because its leaders *and* grassroots have spent more time obsessing over the presidency than building a genuinely bottom-up movement. Working local campaigns helps build that grassroots infrastructure. It will also help us elect more progressives at the local level, allowing us to win today—and build the national bench of tomorrow.

37

INVEST IN DEMOCRACY

RECOMMENDED RESOURCES

DemocracyAlliance.org
IndivisibleGuide.com
SisterDistrict.com
SolidaireNetwork.org
WomenDonors.org

THIS CHAPTER IS for those of you who are donors, and applies to both small-dollar donors and those of you writing five-, six-, and seven-figure checks. You see, there is a deep problem in the way we fund our movement, and it has cost us dearly. Like, "Oh shit, Donald Trump is president" dearly.

The problem: we love to fund organizations that support our favorite *issues*, but we're less passionate about funding the electoral infrastructure that would help *win on those issues*. There is a reflexive, antipartisan bent to broader liberalism, with its focus on issue expertise, policy perfectionism, and other principles of the Enlightenment, but that same liberalism recoils at the crass, street-fighting nature of electoral politics. You know, the kind of politics that wins elections.

This plays out among many of the philanthropists who support progressive, issue-oriented organizations. Instead of funding explicitly partisan operations, we fund so-called 501(c)(3) tax-exempt organizations, or "nonprofits," so called for their tax code classification. And while these organizations can advocate for their *issues* to their hearts' content, they are mostly prohibited from engaging in partisan politics. And liberal donors like that prohibition!

As one big donor told Markos as she rejected his fund-raising solicitation, she didn't want to receive "angry phone calls in the middle of the night." Yet she also happened to be a major donor to pro-choice organizations. In her mind, partisan politics were somehow scarier and nastier than abortion politics!

THOSE SOOTHING TONES OF THE POLITICAL MILQUETOAST

Consider how we, as a movement, prefer the cool, soothing objectivity of NPR to the stridency of a Fox News or *Daily Kos*. We consider ourselves better for consuming "both sides of the issue" journalism at the *New York Times*, when that same publication undermines our political objectives with crappy, falsely "balanced" political reporting and publishes climate-change deniers in its editorial pages. We as liberals desperately want to find "common ground" and "engage in dialogues," convinced that our superior command of facts and figures will carry the day with conservatives who just need to be convinced of . . . something. It's still not clear what.

This focus on issues over infrastructure means that we are hyper-smart about technocratic policy . . . and poorly prepared to win elections.

THE FOCUS ON ISSUES OVER INFRASTRUCTURE MEANS THAT WE ARE HYPERSMART ABOUT TECHNOCRATIC POLICY . . . AND POORLY PREPARED TO WIN ELECTIONS.

Meanwhile, while we fret over purist objectivity in everything, conservatives have built a sophisticated, deeply partisan infrastructure: training institutes to develop their future leaders; college intern recruitment programs; partisan think tanks that pump out conservative messages wrapped in pleasant, centrist-sounding fluff; an entire media ecosystem to distribute, echo, and amplify those messages; electorally minded political advocacy organizations to mobilize and turn out their voters. These organizations, funded with *hundreds of millions of dollars*, have one purpose—Republican victory at the ballot box. They may suck at governing, but boy, can they win! (The exact opposite of us.)

There is absolutely nothing like it on our side. Sure, a lot of money was dumped into Hillary Clinton's coffers in 2016 (and Bernie Sanders' too), but little of that built any lasting infrastructure that can aid Democrats in future elections.

Meanwhile, the Democracy Alliance—a loose coalition of big-money Democratic donors—has mostly pumped money into national organizations focused on big liberal issue priorities like climate change and campaign finance reform. Those same organizations bet big that those *issues* would drive voters to the polls but came up empty. It doesn't matter that people tell pollsters they support efforts to curtail climate change. Issues don't bring out voters. Electoral infrastructure and local organizing do.

**ISSUES DON'T BRING OUT VOTERS.
ELECTORAL INFRASTRUCTURE AND LOCAL
ORGANIZING DO.**

Republicans know this, which is why they don't care about their issues (like "family values," ha ha) when they're on the campaign trail. They are organized and structured *to win elections*. Democrats have nothing like it.

So in the end, a loser like Donald Trump, a candidate with no knowledge of policy or government and no real political campaign to speak of, beat a seasoned, expert policy wonk of a candidate with a massive, well-funded campaign machine.

TIME TO INVEST—IN WINNING ELECTIONS

We've talked in previous chapters about the ninety-seven million voters who did not engage in 2016, and yet for some insane reason, liberal donors aren't spending tens of millions registering voters in Florida, Georgia, Texas, Arizona, or *anywhere else*. They are not spending money on the groups that work directly in marginalized communities who *could* have success increasing voter participation. Big-dollar donors (who are mostly white) don't give money to people of color. They don't know them or trust them to spend the money well. So they squander opportunity after opportunity.

None of this should suggest that issue groups are somehow in the wrong or shouldn't be funded. That's far from the truth, and in fact, the more money they have, the better! Furthermore, many of our best issue advocacy groups do invest heavily in voter mobilization, like NARAL and the League of Conservation Voters. What we need is to build an electorally minded ecosystem of progressive organizations that performs better—that is, gets better results—than the infrastructure the Right has built. That means funding leadership institutes, media, and voter engagement and mobilization organizations. It means funding the new generation of partisan, electoral-minded groups emerging out of the Resistance, like Indivisible and Sister District.

Overall, it means overcoming our inherent fear of partisanship and realizing that the only way we win is to beat the conservative partisan machine.

Then, and *only* then, will we be in a position to win on our issues.

38

TAKE OVER YOUR LOCAL PARTY

RECOMMENDED RESOURCES

Democratic National Committee
Democrats.com
OurRevolution.com
Progressive Democrats America
WeWillReplaceYou.org

WHEN PEOPLE WALK into the voting booth to make their electoral choices, only two parties matter—the Republican one and the Democratic one. Yet we are so frustrated with our party that we badmouth it every chance we get. Who needs Republicans when we ourselves are doing such a good job trashing our own party's brand?

On the other hand, we *are* right. Our party is shit. It is still run by old-school politicos incapable of tapping into the energy generated by the Resistance. It failed to capture grassroots excitement over a round of early 2017 special elections. It failed to even field a chairperson candidate promising real reform (they were all supporters of the status quo, including Bernie Sanders–backed Keith Ellison and eventual winner Tom Perez). It is still infested with political consultants great at wasting donor money but terrible at actually winning elections. Many of its elected officials still pretend that Donald Trump and the Republican Party are a legitimate opposition, afraid of all-out resistance. And it carries the stench of a broken brand.

"We have to take over the Democratic Party," said Michael Moore, speaking at the Women's March. "God bless the Democrats who fought with us. Who've done so many good things. It's no knock on them, but . . . We've won, and then lost. We have let this happen twice now in sixteen years where we win the White House, but they walk through the door." So yes, we have plenty to be frustrated with about the party.

YOU CAN'T WIN IF YOU DON'T PLAY

But the Democratic Party also isn't the caricature relied upon by so many political purists. It's not some faceless "establishment" behemoth. I know it's easy to frame the Resistance movement as standing up to this corporatist monster, but that is not 100 percent accurate. The party is really made up of ordinary people, pretty much just like you. The difference? They showed up—not just once, or even five times, but at the dozens of meetings and conferences and organizing events that are, in fact, "the Democratic Party."

And in politics, showing up means you have a great deal of say in how the party operates. The 2016 Democratic Party platform was, without a doubt, the most progressive in history. While many Sanders supporters kvetched, fact was, the party had adopted the Sanders agenda (some of which was new, but much of which had been a priority for party activists for many years). In early 2017, Democratic leaders were working with Sanders to incorporate his economic populism into the party's 2018 electoral platform.

Thanks to fierce grassroots pressure, Democratic senators stood strong on the Gorsuch nomination to the Supreme Court, and their refusal to deal with Republicans stymied their early attempts to gut Obamacare and replace it with Trumpcare. This is a Democratic Party that no longer flirts with slashing Social Security "to save it" and is standing firm against Republican attacks on entitlements. And remember, this is now an unapologetically pro-gay-rights party when just twelve years ago, Vermont governor Howard Dean was considered *craaaazy* for supporting civil unions!

So there is progress, and it's happening for one reason—you are putting on the pressure. The party hasn't come willingly along—on any of it. Not the Social Security stuff, not the gay rights stuff, not the transgender stuff, not the war stuff back in the day. It's happening because we're taking over the party, and we're doing so by being loud, engaged, and uncompromising. What else can we do?

1. *Literally* **take over the party.** That's exactly what happened in California, with Sanders supporters turning out en masse for otherwise quiet party caucus elections, winning a clear majority of state party delegates. According to Our Revolution, the successor organization of Bernie Sanders' presidential campaign, the Sanders movement fielded over eight hundred delegate candidates, and Our Revolution sent out over one hundred thousand emails and forty thousand texts encouraging people to turn out. In fact, it was almost laughably easy to stage a coup

of this sort—people merely showed up. Given the low turnout typical in such internal affairs, a few hundred people can usually get the job done.

2. **Focus on primaries.** We have a ton of bad Democrats in elected office. We have to get rid of them if we want a better party. Don't listen to people who argue that primaries are divisive and divert resources from taking out Republicans. The Tea Party did a great job cleaning house with Republicans they didn't like, then took over the rest of the government in short order. One note of caution: Democrats in deep-red districts or states should get some leeway to reflect their constituents. As long as they don't publicly undermine the broader party, focus on bad Dems on friendlier turf.

3. **Quit with the third-party stuff.** The party belongs to people who show up. Those who refuse to participate because of the boogeyman "establishment," or who vote third party because they want to "vote their conscience," are forfeiting their right to shape one of the only two parties that matter. As the Tea Party proved, it's easier to take over an existing party than it is to start a new one. And that third party some of you are pining for? What makes you think everyone else wants the same thing? Third party doesn't equal "the party that wants exactly what I want."

4. **Get our nonvoting base to vote.** The party, and its candidates, would look a lot different if we could engage our low-performing base demographics. Politicians will cater to the likeliest voters. Let's make our unlikely voters into likely ones.

We all have two options. Either we complain about the party or we become the party. The latter is more likely to get results.

39

FIX OUR RIGGED SYSTEM

RECOMMENDED RESOURCES
ACLU.org
BrennanCenter.org
CommonCause.org
MiFamiliaVota.org
Mobilize2020.org
NAACP.org
NationalPopularVote.org
ProjectVote.org

TWICE IN THE last sixteen years, including in 2016, the loser of the national popular vote ended up in the White House . . . because our system of "democracy" is crazy. Ironically, the Electoral College, designed to prevent an unqualified person from assuming office, has twice enabled unqualified candidates to become president—Dick Cheney's puppet, George W. Bush, and the weak loser currently infesting the White House right now.

In the Senate, the forty-eight Democrats in the minority have collectively received twenty-three million more votes than the fifty-two Republicans in the majority. Why? Because by design, the Senate is a deeply undemocratic institution, ignoring the notion of proportional representation for . . . reasons (something about being a "great deliberative body"? Last we checked, Mitch McConnell was in charge. Try using the word "great" next to his name).

In state legislatures across the country, the upper chamber is always drawn using districts with equal populations. But nationally, because of Founding Father compromises, each state gets equal treatment in the Senate, whether it has a population of less than one million (as seven states do), or whether it's got more than twenty-five million, such as California and Texas. A logical system would redraw the Senate so that more populous states got more representation. Or even better yet, apportion Senate seats the way we apportion House seats (by a state's population).

But we don't have the benefit of a logical system.

A HOUSE, POORLY DIVIDED

In the House, the Republican gerrymander is so severe that Democrats would have to win the House national popular vote by at least seven points to even have a chance of retaking that chamber. That has given us, once again, the perverse spectacle in which Democrats have generally received more collective votes than the Republican majority throughout this decade, yet they've remained in the deep minority.

Given the demographic shifts already under way, we're headed to a future in which Democrats receive an ever-growing share of the vote—and have to submit to Republican governance.

That's dangerous. We're already seeing the threat of the insatiable Republican thirst for power.

As the GOP rapidly loses national support, it has engaged in an aggressive effort to disenfranchise voters. And they're continuing to focus on blocking voters—voters of color in particular—in spite of numerous court rulings against them.

An appeals court ruling on a North Carolina disenfranchisement effort said that "using race as a proxy for party may be an effective way to win an election. But intentionally targeting a particular race's access to the franchise because its members vote for a particular party, in a predictable manner, constitutes discriminatory purpose. This is so even absent any evidence of race-based hatred and despite the obvious political dynamics." In other words, Tar Heel Republicans were out-and-out racist. How racist? They literally said, out loud, that they were eliminating a day of Sunday voting because "counties with Sunday voting in 2014 were disproportionately black" and "disproportionately Democratic."

"USING RACE AS A PROXY FOR PARTY MAY BE AN EFFECTIVE WAY TO WIN AN ELECTION. BUT INTENTIONALLY TARGETING A PARTICULAR RACE'S ACCESS TO THE FRANCHISE . . . CONSTITUTES DISCRIMINATORY PURPOSE."

They didn't even bother hiding their racism!

Another court in Texas, rolling back a similar voter disenfranchisement effort there, ruled in January 2017: "The record shows that drafters and proponents of SB14 were aware of the likely disproportionate effect of the law on minorities, and that they nonetheless passed the bill without adopting a number of proposed ameliorative measures that might have lessened this impact."

A court in Wisconsin ruled in July 2016: "Republicans sought to maintain control of the state government. But the methods that the legislature chose to achieve that result involved suppressing the votes of Milwaukee's residents, who are disproportionately African-American and Latino. . . . That, too, constitutes race discrimination."

Despite these legal setbacks, thirty-four states had similar restrictive laws on their books as of early 2017. So what can we do to fix our democracy?

1. **Support the National Popular Vote Compact.** States are allowed to distribute their electoral votes as they see fit. With the compact, states give their electoral votes to the winner of the popular vote, but it doesn't take effect until enough states to equal 270 electoral votes pass the compact. As of early 2017, that number stood at 160 electoral votes. If your state doesn't support it yet, lobby your state legislature to pass it. And yes, it's constitutional, and no, it doesn't require a constitutional amendment.

2. **Support statehood for Puerto Rico and Washington, DC.** DC has a larger population than Vermont and Wyoming, yet its residents have *zero* representation in Congress (one nonvoting member in the House doesn't count). This travesty must end. Puerto Rico has internal politics to sort out, but if island residents agree that they want statehood, the nation should grant it. We could get fanciful and advocate splitting California into two states, maybe smooshing the Dakotas into one state, but as much as that would highlight the absurdity of our current system . . . not going to happen. Let's start with the low-hanging fruit first.

THE RESISTANCE HANDBOOK: 45 WAYS TO FIGHT TRUMP

3. **Beat back Republican gerrymanders.** Statewide elections in 2018 will elect many of the governors and legislators who will draw district boundaries after the 2020 census reapportionment (go reread the chapter on protecting the census). Let's win these races! We don't need full control of redistricting commissions to win. Even one veto point (like a governor) would kick redistricting to the courts, which would then draw fair maps. And with fair maps, it's not just Democrats who win, but all the American people.

4. **Support organizations fighting racist voter laws.** The NAACP, the ACLU, MALDEF, and others are on the legal front lines. Financially support their efforts. If you are a lawyer, consider this your pro bono work.

5. **Fight for felon reenfranchisement**. According to the Sentencing Project, 2.5 percent of all Americans are barred from voting because of a past felony conviction. That number is almost 8 percent for African-Americans, or one in thirteen. In Florida, nearly a quarter of African-Americans cannot vote. Many of those felonies are bullshit low-level drug offenses and plea bargains, but even when the convictions are for legit crimes, former prisoners who have served their time have done their just penance. There is no public policy benefit to continuing to deny them a political voice other than partisan advantage for Republicans.

6. **Advocate for vote-by-mail.** There are people who hold romantic ideals about voting in a ballot box on Election Day. Those people are all white and don't live in urban districts. It is no accident that suburban voters can be in and out on Election Day in fifteen minutes, while urban voters must wait in line for hours to vote. Republican election officials will overload their

favorable districts with machines and create "voting deserts"—places where it's nearly impossible to vote—in areas in which Democratic voters are dominant. With vote-by-mail, there are no lines to wait in, there are no trolls to challenge voting credentials, there are no IDs to show, there are no artificial restrictions the GOP can place in the path of traditionally liberal voters. California, Colorado, Oregon, and Washington all do either full vote-by-mail or mostly so, and there have been no reported cases of fraud. It is safe, secure, convenient, and inclusionary. No wonder Republicans hate it.

7. **Advocate for automatic voter registration.** The idea of registering to vote is ludicrous. People should be automatically enrolled when getting any sort of ID at the DMV, or better yet, automatically when they turn eighteen. For those who have religious (or other) objections to being registered, an opt-out can be provided.

Absent a severe constitutional overhaul, we are stuck with this imperfect system. It is our job to mitigate those barriers to the fullest extent possible. But also remember—a primary reason these restrictions are harming us at the ballot box is because of those ninety-seven million Americans who do not vote.

Racist laws and felon disenfranchisement could be overturned at the state level if we won those elections. Laws could be passed making it easier for everyone to vote (even Republicans!). Districts could be fairly drawn.

So let's get our people to vote! And let's also make sure their vote counts.

40

RUN FOR OFFICE/ RECRUIT CANDIDATES

RECOMMENDED RESOURCES

314Action.org
BrandNewCongress.org
EmergeAmerica.org
EMILYs List
Flippable.org
OnlyIfYou.run
RunforSomething.net
SheShouldRun.org
SisterDistrict.com
SwingLeft.org
VoteRunLead.org
Wellstone.org

IN THE FINAL address of his presidency, as much of the nation watched in distress and fear, President Barack Obama gamely tried to rally his distressed supporters. "If you're disappointed by your elected officials," he said, "grab a clipboard, get some signatures, and run for office yourself. Show up. Dive in."

That's certainly been a tough sell in recent years. Few people want to face the heightened media scrutiny. Others have other career goals. But most simply haven't seen politics as worth engaging in.

And then there is the drudgery everyone running for office faces— the degrading, never-ending phone calls begging for campaign contributions, life on the road away from family and loved ones, pretending the wealthy folks writing checks at big-dollar fundraisers are all super interesting (some are, many are not, a bunch are simply assholes). Your odds of winning as a Democrat haven't been great of late, and if you win, your "reward" is to move away from your home to either DC or a remote state capital, like Springfield, Albany, or Sacramento. For most, the hassle is just not worth it.

That dearth of new talent, along with the electoral decimation of the Obama years, means the Democratic leadership is old and ossified. At the beginning of 2017, House Democratic leader Nancy Pelosi was seventy-seven, Bernie Sanders was seventy-five, Joe Biden was seventy-four, Elizabeth Warren was sixty-seven, Senate minority leader Chuck Schumer was sixty-six. The top three Democrats in the House were all at least seventy-five. The three highest-ranking Democrats after Schumer in the Senate are all older than him.

These are all great leaders, and Warren in particular is a powerful spokesperson for the Democratic Left. But they would be the first to acknowledge the need for the party's elected ranks to get younger and more relevant to the party's base demographics. Yet there is currently no bench from which to draw future Democratic candidates for higher office.

NOTHING MOTIVATES LIKE A CRISIS

Donald Trump has certainly changed that, making concerns about career and scrutiny suddenly seem small or insignificant. Our country faces an existential threat, and people are stepping up to do something about it. They're not waiting for the party to give them a call (those people are only interested in self-funding millionaires anyway).

The organization Run for Something has signed up over eight thousand millennials interested in running for office since launching in January 2017. "If we want to see change, the best way we can make it is to run for office," Heather Ward, a twenty-one-year-old senior at Villanova University who is running for a school board seat near Philadelphia, told *Time*. "Making phone calls to representatives is great. But it's the people in those offices who make the decisions." Wise, and accurate.

VoteRunLead, which focuses on training women candidates, had nearly sixty-five hundred women take its online course between the November 2016 elections and April of 2017. In that same time period, She Should Run went from several dozen potential candidates taking their online course per month, to over eight thousand. During all of the 2016 cycle, EMILY's List, which recruits and supports women candidates, fielded inquiries from nine hundred candidates, total. In the first four months of 2017, that number had surpassed *eleven thousand.*

This heightened interest is amazing—and we urgently need to sustain it. Not only is the party in desperate need of younger, more diverse, and more progressive candidates, but there may never be a better time to run than now. Data from the early 2017 special elections found Democratic candidates running around *twenty points* stronger than Donald Trump's numbers. It didn't matter if the races were in rural white districts or suburban white ones or urban ones or Latino ones. It didn't matter if it was a mayor's race, a state legislative one, or a congressional special election.

Thanks to the Trump effect, in all cases, the Democratic vote was strong, while the Republican one was depressed. That vote shift is so dramatic, in fact, that if that same gap maintains through November 2018, fully *124 Republican-held congressional seats could be in danger*. Not all of them will be in play, of course. But as of early 2017, we needed only 24 seats to take control of the chamber. In a normal gerrymandered House? That would be a tall order. In today's anti-Trump climate, all bets are off. And the more we succeed in making Trump toxic, the worse down-ballot Republicans will fare.

THE "TOXIC TRUMP EFFECT" MEANS THERE'S NEVER BEEN A BETTER TIME TO RUN AS A DEMOCRAT.

Things are looking so good for us, in fact, that Democrats may be en route to one-upping the GOP's rout in 2010 when they won 63 House seats and an eye-watering 720 state legislative seats. That year, Republicans flipped what was a 60–39 Democratic advantage in state legislatures to a Republican 59–40 edge. (Today, it's 68–31 Republicans.) But we won't see numbers like those unless we have strong, energetic candidates up and down the ballot.

1. **RUN! Or have that amazing person in your life run.** Whether it's you or someone in your orbit who you think is spectacular, prioritize finding and recruiting candidates.
2. **Connect with national allies.** Run for Something is focusing on candidates under the age of thirty-five. 314 Action is working to get scientists to run for office (get it? π?). *Daily Kos* is always looking for good primary challengers to Democrats who are demonstrably more conservative than the demographics of their districts or states, as well as general election challengers in

state and federal races. Wellstone Action does candidate trainings. Emerge America focuses on women candidates, while EMILY's List helps fund them. PowerPAC works with candidates of color. Flippable helps state-level candidates. Sister District Project matches volunteers in safe blue and red districts with campaigns in competitive races.

3. **Connect with local activism groups.** Find your local activism groups, such as Indivisible chapters, Democratic Party clubs, etc. Solicit volunteers and support. Network at meetings you normally wouldn't attend, and build yourself a staff and core cadre of volunteers that reflect the demographics of your district.

4. **Don't expect the party to help.** If you happen to be in a top-tier race, then you'll get showered with money . . . along with some of the party's shitty consultants. It's a double-edged sword. But odds are, you won't be running for one of those seats, so focus on doing things yourself, in conjunction with local resistance groups and allies. The party can be the bonus, but it should never form your core.

The election cycles of 2018 and 2020 will be hugely important for us. Not only do we have a historic opportunity to roll back the GOP gains of the 2010s from the bottom up, but we can do so in a way that remakes our party, turning it younger, more progressive, and more reflective of our nation's demographics. And we need you to help make it happen. So remember, consider running, or help us find those amazing candidates.

BUILD GRASSROOTS INFRASTRUCTURE

41

BE THE MEDIA

RECOMMENDED RESOURCES

Crook and Liars
Facebook
FAIR.org
Media Matters
PantSuitNation.org
RightWingWatch.org
SourceWatch.org

Subscribe:
American Prospect
E—The Environmental Magazine
In These Times
Mother Jones
The Nation
The Progressive
Utne Reader
Washington Monthly

THE STATE OF the American news media is, to put it mildly, *complicated.* There are the old, traditional media institutions and the newer (mostly conservative) partisan ones. There is the democratizing force of *social* media, and we can now add the scourge of *fake* media. Let's take a look at each.

The first is the traditional media—newspapers and television news that are pretending to be "objective" but are really just awful. These are the people who had dozens of reporters trying to find nonexistent dirt on Hillary Clinton's emails and the Clinton Family Foundation. And sure, they never found anything, but that didn't stop them from writing endless articles full of baseless innuendo and insinuations. Led by the execrable CNN, this is also the same traditional media that gave Donald Trump $5.6 *billion* (with a "b") in free, "earned" media, according to data from media tracking firm mediaQuant. Another study by social media analytics company Crimson Hexagon found that Clinton didn't just receive the most negative media coverage online in media outlets like CNN, Fox News, the *Washington Post, Politico,* and the *New York Times,* but she also received the lowest number of positive stories—about half those that Trump got.

In fact, Clinton overcame Trump's massive media-coverage advantage only twice during the campaign—when she fainted at a campaign stop, and when FBI director James Comey released the infamous letter about the investigation into the fake email "scandal." This was the same media obsessed with false equivalencies, such as ABC News chief political analyst Matthew Dowd tweeting: "Either you care both about Trump being sexual predator & Clinton emails, or u care about neither. But don't talk about one without the other." Utter bullcrap.

A study for Harvard's Shorenstein Center on Media, Politics and Public Policy found that "stories about her personal traits portrayed her as overly cautious and guarded and ran 3-to-1 negative. News reports on her policy positions trended negative by a ratio of 4-to-1. Everything from her position on health care to her position on trade was criticized, often in the form of an attack by Trump or another opponent. Her record of public service, which conceivably should have been a source of positive press, turned out differently. News reports on that topic were 62 percent negative to 38 percent positive, with Trump having a larger voice than she did in defining the meaning of her career. He was widely quoted as saying, 'She's been there 30 years and has nothing to show for it.'"

NYU journalism professor Jay Rosen (follow him on Twitter!) has a phrase that describes the sorry state of supposedly impartial traditional American political journalism. He calls it "the view from nowhere":

> In pro journalism, American style, the View from Nowhere is a bid for trust that advertises the viewlessness of the news producer. Frequently it places the journalist between polarized extremes, and calls that neither-nor position "impartial." Second, it's a means of defense against a style of criticism that is fully anticipated: charges of bias originating in partisan politics and the two-party system. Third: it's an attempt to secure a kind of universal legitimacy that is implicitly denied to those who stake out positions or betray a point of view. American journalists have almost a lust for the View from Nowhere because they think it has more authority than any other possible stance.

Yes, yes, conservatives like to call the traditional media "liberal," and some liberals actually believe it! But that's what we call gaslighting. The traditional media are not liberal allies, any more so than Fox News is. Remember that. These media outlets aren't here to help us. What can you do about this?

1. **Don't subscribe to media organizations that promote right-wing voices and propaganda.** Why should you send *your* hard-earned dollars to publications that allow themselves to be used as propaganda platforms by the Right?

2. **Respond to media bias.** Whether it's a letter to the editor for a newspaper (they still matter!) or dropping a comment into a publication's toxic stew of a comments section, it's important to challenge conservatives and right-wing tropes whenever and wherever they arise.

3. **Follow media-bias trackers like Media Matters and Right Wing Watch.** These services provide important insight into the right-wing dominance of our media ecosystem. Share their findings with your social networks.

4. **Use Twitter to challenge journalists.** Twitter allows direct access to most journalists, so let them know when they write biased stories, as well as thank them when they practice real journalism.

5. **Share good articles on social media.** There are good writers at almost every traditional publication. Share their material on social media. The more clicks those individuals get, the more space they have inside their organizations to write the good stuff, and the better the placement of their material.

6. **Don't expect traditional media outlets to "help" us.** That's not their job. Only we can help ourselves.

7. **Establish relationships with local media.** Those outlets will generally be more approachable than national ones. Offer tips and other assistance to reporters working the political beat.

Make any criticism constructive. Keep them abreast of the work your activism group is doing.

The second media category: partisan news outlets. Conservatives have spent decades and billions establishing the building blocks of their partisan media ecosystem—Fox News, the *Wall Street Journal* editorial board (and many of its reporters), the *Washington Times*, Rush Limbaugh and virtually all of AM radio, Drudge Report, Glenn Beck, the *Weekly Standard*, *National Review*, *Free Republic*, and the conservative blogosphere; they even badger Congress into threatening NPR's funding, which had the desired effect of tilting NPR to the right (this is a tactic known as "working the refs").

But even *all that* wasn't enough, so in more recent years they spent tens of millions building up Breitbart, as well as other white-supremacist conservative online outlets. Meanwhile, the Left has a few hours on MSNBC (their mornings are owned by conservative Joe Scarborough), *Daily Kos*, and . . . that might be it. What was once a thriving liberal blogosphere was decimated by the refusal of liberals to fund liberal media. A sad effort at a radio presence, Air America, was felled by incompetence. While *Daily Kos* has been surging since Trump's election, this is a space mostly dominated by conservative forces. So what can you do about it?

1. **Patronize quality liberal *partisan* sites.** *Vox* and *Huffington Post* both practice quality journalism with a liberal slant. *Daily Kos* provides unapologetically liberal news analysis. Visit and support liberal blogs like Crooks and Liars and Wonkette, and partisan news outlets like Raw Story.
2. **Support those sites!** Online advertising pays shit. If you find a blogger or site that you like, support them with cold, hard cash.

THE RESISTANCE HANDBOOK: 45 WAYS TO FIGHT TRUMP

3. Boycott brands that support right-wing news personalities.
Fox News ratings leader Bill O'Reilly didn't lose his job because of his sexual harassment and assaults—according to multiple women, that's apparently a feature of working for Rupert Murdoch. He got ousted (with a $20 million payday) because ordinary viewers took it upon themselves to boycott advertisers who supported O'Reilly's predatory misogyny. As the ad revenues bled out the door, Fox News had no choice but to dump the host. And if you're worried about the tactic being turned against liberal partisan publishers, don't worry. Big brands have avoided us for years. They have long been more afraid of conservative activists than liberal ones.

Next up in the ecosystem: fake news—that new media genre entirely focused on feeding our hunger for ideologically affirming conspiracy theories. A toxic stew of greedy click-bait "entrepreneurs" and Russian intelligence now feeds idiot conservatives with outright bullshit. The truth is irrelevant as long as their worldview is validated. Note that at least one election-season fake news purveyor tried his hand with liberal fake news, only to fail miserably. "We've tried to do similar things to liberals," Jestin Coler told NPR. "It just has never worked, it never takes off. You'll get debunked within the first two comments and then the whole thing just kind of fizzles out." That doesn't mean that liberals are immune, we're not, so we must always remain vigilant on our own side.

But conservatives fell, en masse, for headlines such as "Pope Francis shocks world, endorses Donald Trump for president" (960,000 "engagements" on Facebook, defined as "post clicks, likes, shares and comments"), "Donald Trump sent his own plane to transport 200 stranded marines" (893,000 engagements), and "WikiLeaks confirms Hillary sold weapons to ISIS . . . Then drops another bombshell" (shared 789,000 times). It wasn't even that they were too stupid to figure out that those headlines were false. *They simply didn't care* one way or another. All that mattered was that it validated their biases.

Here's how to fight fake news:

1. **Don't believe everything you read.** Believe it or not, stuff on the Internet is sometimes wrong. If the headline seems crazy, chances are it might be. The more incredible the claim, the more skeptically you should approach it.

2. **Check sourcing.** See who is reporting the news. If you've never heard of it, be skeptical. Look at sources in the story. Are there any? If not, it's a red flag. Are sources anonymous? Another red flag.

3. **Wait for confirmation.** *Daily Kos* always waits for multiple news outlets to report a piece of news before accepting it as true. Even if the news outlet is legit, waiting for confirmation never hurt anyone. Even good journalists sometimes screw up.

4. **Make sure the story is not parody.** You don't want to be *that* person who takes an *Onion* or Andy Borowitz story seriously.

5. **Do not share a story until it is confirmed!** Fun fact: most people don't read the stories they share. They see a headline, they agree with it, then they share. Please put a little more thought into it.

Finally, there's the most democratic (small "d") of all media—social media. Publishing—what was once the province of those who owned printing presses and "bought ink by the barrel"—is now available to any schlub with a computer or mobile device. And that will always be amazing, no matter how many neofascist conservatives take to Twitter and Facebook to spew their Nazi bile.

The reason: whatever the Right does with these powerful tools, we can do even better. There are more of us. We have creativity, diversity, inclusivity, and youth on our side. Our ideas are more popular. And it's our people creating these technologies in the first place! The greatest irony of the social media era is watching conservatives rail against "liberal" San Francisco, New York, Austin, Boston, and Seattle . . . on social media, which was largely created in those cities.

In May 2016, a Pew study found that liberals were far more likely to receive election news from Facebook than conservatives (51 percent to 34 percent). And let's face it, the millennials and Generation Y folks who are the future of our party and our movement are far more adept at social media than the old white men who make up the bulk of the dying Republican Party.

Resistance groups rapidly adopted many of these tools as they worked to get off the ground. Indivisible began as a simple Google doc full of great information. Pantsuit Nation began as a private Facebook group, and then a network of local private Facebook groups. #Black Lives Matter is called that specifically because it launched (and still generates a great deal of its activism) on Twitter.

So, how does a Resistance fighter make the most of social media?

1. **Politicize your social interactions.** There should be no separation between your "personal" social media accounts and your activism. They are one and the same. Don't be afraid to be political as you communicate to the world.

2. **Publish.** The social web is full of options for anyone with something to say, and if you're reading this book, you probably (hopefully) have something to say. Twitter lets you be short and pithy. *Daily Kos* and Medium offer longer-form self-publishing solutions. Tumblr is somewhere in the middle. Facebook allows

you to focus on your more familiar network. Pick one or more of these outlets and . . .

3. **Share, share, share.** There are amazing people doing amazing work. There are terrible people trying to destroy what we hold dear. These are all stories worth sharing (fake news caveat aside). The more informed our fellow activists, the smarter, more effective we will be.

4. **Use video.** Standing Rock protesters made incredible use of Livestream to beam images of their work to millions of devices around the country. Facebook Live, Periscope, and other similar tools turn everyone's devices into little broadcast studios. The effect can be quite powerful.

5. **Jujitsu conservative tactics.** After a federal judge in Hawaii blocked Trump's second attempt at a Muslim travel ban, outraged conservatives launched the hashtag #BoycottHawaii to express their displeasure. After gaining some traction in the right-wing Twitterverse, liberals, led by Democratic representative Ted Lieu of California, struck back. "#BoycottHawaii is trending. Then it'll be #BoycottMaryland [because of the second] court decision. Soon only place folks can go is Steve King's [conservative Iowa] district," tweeted Lieu. Another tweeted, "You go right ahead and boycott. More room for us humans." A passenger on a flight to Hawaii tweeted a picture of his neighbor wearing a "Trump" sweatshirt, saying, "This Trump supporter didn't get the #boycotthawaii memo . . ." In the face of liberal mocking, the effort died a quick, hilarious death.

While the problems with the traditional media are huge, and seemingly intractable, we *can* use social media to circumvent its limitations. Use it to promote partisan liberal media outlets, so they can better

THE RESISTANCE HANDBOOK: 45 WAYS TO FIGHT TRUMP

balance out the Right's massive media machine. Use it to hold traditional journalists accountable while also supporting those who are doing the important, invaluable work of real journalism. Use it to get the word out about Resistance actions and organizing, helping us build lasting infrastructure to support our movement and its leaders. And use it to share your own political thoughts—because we're willing to bet that you are more interesting and relevant than half the jackasses on the *New York Times* opinion pages.

In other words, don't just sit there and complain about our shitty media, *be the media*.

42

ORGANIZE LOCALLY

RECOMMENDED RESOURCES

The Blueprint: How the Democrats Won Colorado by
    Adam Schrager and Bob Witwer
Drinking Liberally
ForwardMajority.com
Nextdoor.com
ProgressNow.org
TheResistanceParty.org
SolidaritySundays.org
Together We Will
TrumpIntelPro.com
WomensMarch.com

IT WAS NOVEMBER 2002, and progressives throughout Colorado had just been wiped out. The state wasn't just in Republican hands, but in the hands of the worst kind of Republicans—extreme right-wing nuts whose entire agenda was bashing gays and getting the Ten Commandments placed in public schools.

Colorado progressives licked their wounds, then began plotting their comeback. They gathered a small group willing to fight this hateful agenda. First step? Michael Huttner set up a messaging war room, complete with a blog and an email list targeting seven hundred of his colleagues and friends. At first, the blog and email list focused on calling out the Right's lack of ethics, their corruption, and their placement of partisan politics above the people.

Next, Michael tapped into several veterans of the Howard Dean campaign, bringing in money and digital organizing chops. Over ten months, they developed a technology platform that not only allowed top-down, one-to-many online email blasts, but also provided the tools for people to organize their own local communities around the issues they cared about. And thus, ProgressNow was born. (Not too long after, in early 2007, that team used this very same platform for then-senator Barack Obama's first presidential run.)

RED TO PURPLE, PURPLE TO BLUE

Several years after launch, that original seven-hundred-person email list had grown to tens of thousands. Over the following decade, ProgressNow played a pivotal role in turning Colorado from blood-red to a purplish-to-blue progressive state. While so many other Obama states backslid into Trump's column in 2016, Colorado held firm for Hillary Clinton. Meanwhile, the ProgressNow model was expanded to twenty-three other states, and the network boasts a combined three million members today—all focused on transforming the politics of their state. As famed anthropologist Margaret Mead once said, "Never doubt that a small group of thoughtful, committed citizens can change the world—indeed, it's the only thing that ever has." And that is never more possible than at the local level.

We have reinforced, in chapter after chapter, the importance of organizing locally. It is at the local level that policy impacts us most directly—from the condition of the roads we drive, to the quality and funding of our schools, to our ability to cast our vote. Yet progressives appear to care little about their own political backyard. That's why despite the fact that Democrats held a majority of state legislatures when Obama took office, Republicans systematically decimated Democratic ranks at the local level. At the start of 2017, only fifteen of the nation's governors were Democratic. They held a majority in just thirty-one out of ninety-eight state legislative chambers. They lost over eight hundred state legislative seats total during Obama's term, and lost every single Southern legislative chamber for the first time in history.

Of course, none of that was an accident. Conservative donors poured tens of millions of dollars into those races every cycle, crushing by comparison the relatively puny contributions of liberal donors. Those conservatives spent $30 million in 2010, and $38 million in 2014. Democrats barely cracked $10 million. Meanwhile, the Koch brothers and other conservative donors poured millions more into building state-based grassroots infrastructure and funding the Tea Party groups that emerged in the wake of the Democrats' messy and contentious 2009–2010 health care debate.

THE PROGRESSIVE OBSESSION

Meanwhile, liberals were busy obsessing about one single unitary office: the presidency. The Democratic Party was burning at the state level, and liberals argued over whether Obama was progressive enough (also known as the "rox vs. sux" battles). Governorships and state legislatures were falling like dominoes to the GOP, and liberals obsessed over whether Bernie Sanders or Hillary Clinton was the "real" progressive.

Republican majorities decimated local unions, enacted barriers to voting, implemented harsh restrictions on choice, and blocked health care for their residents, and liberals could not be bothered to pay attention!

The playing field is so tilted toward the GOP now that even a President Bernie Sanders would be unable to accomplish much; a White House mandate is only as powerful as its influence in Congress. That debate is academic, anyway, because that GOP dominance at the grassroots level helped deliver them the White House. They won because we, as liberals, were focused on the wrong thing. So now we have to do everything we can to rebuild our local infrastructure.

1. **Join organizations focused on local politics.** Organizations like ProgressNow and its state partners are laser-focused on statewide issues. Find these organizations and join them.

2. **Start or join local offline activism groups.** We've already talked about the great work Indivisible is doing. There are many other similar groups. Find the ones in your area and get engaged.

3. **Support great candidates or run yourself!** We've already discussed the importance of rebuilding our bench from the ground up. Find people to run for everything, even if it's the library board or dogcatcher! (Fun fact: there are no elected dogcatchers in the country . . .)

4. **Wage local politics.** Help local campaigns: spread the word in local newspapers, websites, and social networks like Next-Door, or even leaflet a busy downtown corner. If people aren't motivated to vote in national elections, perhaps local ones could provide better motivation. Go to city council meetings and make your voice heard on local matters.

5. **Talk, talk, talk about these issues** to everyone around you. People are conditioned not to care about local politics. You are

the person who can change that. And remember how powerful door-to-door canvassing is? Yeah, do *that*, even if it's just your immediate neighbors or your block.

6. **Join and/or take over your local party.** Remember, the Democratic Party isn't this monolithic beast. It's a patchwork of smaller state and local parties. If yours is effectively run, join and help its efforts. If it's not, take it over. Really, at the most local levels, the person who bothers to show is almost always the person who gets to be in charge.

7. **Support local advocacy orgs and nonprofits.** Local groups do a great deal of organizing around key issues, yet because of their local focus, they have some of the hardest times funding operations. Find the good ones and donate, then host a fundraiser to multiply your donation. If you have a relevant skill set, volunteer your time.

And then, when the next presidential primary battle heats up, feel free to spare a glance and take sides. But the battle that matters most will be in your backyard. The more effective you are in winning your local turf, the more effective national Democrats will be, no matter who ends up in the White House.

43

INCREASE OUR VISIBILITY

RECOMMENDED RESOURCES

FreewayBlogger.com
PlasticJesus.net

YOU MAY HAVE heard of the LA artist Plastic Jesus, who put a tiny wall around Donald Trump's Hollywood star, achieving instant mega-viral fame. Yet his wider splash has been his "No Trump Anywhere" red and white street signs, in the mold of No Parking signs, that have cropped up on city poles all over the country.

"On the most basic level, the idea behind the project was to really show my concerns of Donald Trump possibly becoming the next president of the United States," Plastic Jesus told art site Hyperallergic.

"These street signs are pretty bold and basic in their message, but we need to be basic in the message that we need to get out about Trump."

And what's the best way to reinforce the anti-Trump message to the broader masses? Well, that's easy: blanket the country with anti-Trump messages. Plastering political messages on existing signage is a time-honored tradition—from hagiographic billboards in despotic regimes like Cuba and North Korea, to war propaganda like Rosie the Riveter, to the lawn signs and bumper stickers of American elections today.

THE ARTIST KATSU BUILT A DRONE CAPABLE OF SPRAY-PAINTING THE WORDS "SCUM TRUMP" IN HARD-TO-REACH PLACES. THE ARTIST PLANS TO RELEASE ALL HARDWARE AND SOFTWARE SPECS FOR OTHERS TO ADOPT.

When activists asked the Democratic candidate in an April 2017 US House special election for lawn signs, his campaign balked. Didn't everyone know that lawn signs didn't vote? But activists in this heavily conservative Wichita, Kansas–area district wanted to send a message that even this deep in red territory, Democrats were present and ready to be counted. When the votes were tallied, the Republican still won, but Democrats outpaced their historical performance by *twenty points*—in a mostly rural, mostly white district.

Hiding in the shadows and hoping for the best is not an effective political strategy. It doesn't build that sense of common purpose and community. It doesn't inspire courage or activate your allies. We are the American majority and we need to use every opportunity, every medium at our disposal, to be visible and spread our message. And signage is a great way to do it.

Plastic Jesus got the first batch of "No Trump Anywhere" signs made himself, but has since placed the template online for others to download and use. Another of his downloadable creations is a sign, designed to be placed on the kind of fencing that surrounds empty or abandoned lots, that reads, "Lot reserved for Future Internment Camp by order of Donald J. Trump." Another artist, KATSU, built a drone capable of spray-painting the words "Scum Trump" in hard-to-reach places. The artist plans to release all hardware and software specs for others to adopt.

Patrick Randall, who goes by the name "Freeway Blogger," has put up over seven thousand signs on freeways since 2003 (with zero arrests, he likes to point out). He's now focusing on Resistance-themed messages like "Sadly, treason wouldn't be the ugliest thing about him," "Our new president does seem kind of weird about Russia," and, simply, "Resist." Many of these signs are hung on overpasses, others off to the side of the road, and others piggybacking off existing highway signage—where they get viewed by tens of thousands of motorists every day. His website offers tips on both how to make these big signs and where to place them so they remain up for the longest possible amount of time.

Ultimately, the idea here is to make the message of resistance as visible in the physical world as possible. So some options:

1. **Lawn signs.** If your local campaigns don't have them, you or your local group can get some printed up. It's not too expensive, it signals your neighbors that it's safe to come out if they're liberal, and it opens up avenues of dialogue to those who are receptive to the message. You can also come up with your own Resistance-themed message to display. A simple "Resist!" can do the trick.

2. **Bumper stickers.** Millions of Americans are stuck in traffic for hours every day. It's a great place to reinforce just how hated Trump really is.

3. **Freeway blogging.** Check out the Freeway Blogger website and consider having you or your local activism group give it a shot.

4. **Post signs in public places.** Follow Plastic Jesus' lead and hang Resistance-themed signage in public places. Download his "No Trump Anywhere" and "Internment Camp" templates to have those signs hung in your town. When they get taken down, put new ones up, or find harder-to-reach places for installation.

5. **Wear Resistance-themed apparel.** If the Resistance is a brand, think like brand advertisers. Stick that brand on a T-shirt. Wear T-shirts promoting local campaigns. *Daily Kos* sells Resistance-themed lapel pins in its store.

6. **Fly the symbols of our Resistance allies.** Proudly display the rainbow flag. Put up a Black Lives Matter sign. If your local union is organizing, put up lawn signs. And don't let this be the end of your support, but simply the beginning.

The theme? Put Resistance messaging anywhere you can—at your house, on your car, in your neighborhood, and in the streets. The more pervasive it is, the more inspired our allies will feel to join us in our fight.

44

GET A JOB IN POLITICS

RECOMMENDED RESOURCES

DemocraticGain.org
EnvironmentalCareer.com
FightfortheFuture.org
Idealist.org
NonProfit-Jobs.org
TheNonprofitNetwork.org
PhilanthropyNewsDigest.org
ProgressiveExchange.org
TomManatosJobs.com

MICHAEL AND MARKOS are lucky as hell. We both get to spend our working days doing what we love best—fighting for our country. No matter your skill set, there are myriad political organizations, nonprofit advocacy organizations, party committees, candidates, and forward-thinking companies looking to staff up. Generally speaking, the shared noble mission of these organizations creates a sense of *family* among staff. The goal isn't to increase revenues for investors or the owner, but to improve the lives of people, of animals, of our environment, of our world.

But what about pay? Nonprofits must surely be low on the pay scale, right? Actually, according to a January 2016 report from the US Bureau of Labor Statistics, people working at nonprofit organizations earned *more*, on average, than those working at for-profit companies, and significantly so—$25.30 an hour versus $20.17. That $5.13 premium for nonprofit employees actually grew to $7.86 when including the value of health and retirement benefits. Doing the math . . . forty-hour workweeks . . . carry the one . . . that's just over *$16,000* in increased compensation per year!

Of course, the actual data is a little more complicated—the numbers vary by industry, geographic location, and whether the employee is management or not. But while one might intuitively expect for-profit management to earn significantly higher wages, the reality, according to the data, is that "management, professional, and related workers at nonprofit businesses are seen to earn wages that are 96 percent of the level of their for-profit counterparts." Throw in the value of benefits packages, and "there is no statistical compensation gap between nonprofit and for-profit businesses for management."

So lower-level workers make significantly more than their private-sector counterparts (likely because there is no management incentive to maximize profits on the backs of the labor force), while the top ranks have full parity when including the value of retirement and health benefits.

So you can work doing something you believe in *and* get paid well for it? Where do you sign up?

- **Democratic Gain.** "Democratic GAIN is the association for progressive political professionals and organizations. Our members benefit from our premier job and talent banks; individualized career counseling; and training and certifications."

- **Environmental Career Center.** "The Environmental Career Center provides employers and job seekers with comprehensive career, and staffing services in the environmental, sustainability, natural resources, energy, and green jobs sectors."
- **Idealist.** "Idealist is all about connecting idealists—people who want to do good—with opportunities for action and collaboration. With more than 120,000 organizations and 1.4 million monthly visitors to our English, and Spanish (idealistas.org) sites, Idealist helps people move from intention to action all over the world."
- **NonProfit-Jobs.org.** "Connecting mission-driven talent with organizations important to our civic infrastructure."
- **The Nonprofit Network.** "The Nonprofit Network connects you with hot jobs from today's best not-for-profit employers."
- **Philanthropy News Digest Jobs.** "PND's job board provides listings of current full-time job openings at tax-exempt organizations."
- **Progressive Exchange.** "The Progressive Exchange is an online community that was started as a way to share information about online strategies, tactics and tools among people doing Internet organizing, advocacy, marketing and fundraising on behalf of the public interest."
- **Tom Manatos Jobs.** "Tom Manatos Jobs has helped thousands of people find government and political jobs since 2002. It connects the area's leading employers to qualified job seekers of all levels of experience and expertise."

45

MAKE ACTIONS A PART OF YOUR LIFE

RECOMMENDED RESOURCES

5Calls.org
ActionAlliance.co
DailyAction.org
DailyGrabBack.com
ResistHere.org
RiseStronger.org
SolidaritySundays.org
SwingLeft.org
TrumpResistance.today
Track-Trump.com
Wall-of-Us.org
WhattheFuckJustHappenedToday.com

THERE ARE DOZENS upon dozens of actions we can take to resist Trump and work toward a more just and equitable society. No one should get to this point in this book and wonder, "What else can I do?" The question really becomes, "Given my skill set and interests, which of these should I do today?"

The key is to make activism—and specifically, actions—a part of your lifestyle. Schedule them into your routine as you would shopping, eating, and breathing. Join organizations, like Wall of Us, that feed you a steady diet of new actions to take. Let this become the new normal; do *not* let your activism become a Trump-induced anomaly. So find a pace that is sustainable but constant. This will be a lifelong fight. Conservatives never stop organizing, and neither can we, regardless of which Republican crazy is running their asylum.

Work tirelessly to bring other people into the fold, first as voters, then as activists. It's simple math. The larger our movement, the larger our electorate, the stronger and more effective it will be. Share links and stories and actions with everyone around you. Share this book as well. The larger the menu of available actions, the more likely it is that people will find something they enjoy doing. And have fun! Activism doesn't have to be a grind; in fact, if you're doing it right, it can be among the most rewarding and productive things you'll do with your time.

Remember that, as bad as things might sometimes look, there is love and beauty all around us. Don't forget to reconnect with the things that give you strength and purpose—your family, your god, or hobbies that fulfill you, whether it's music, art, or a hike through the park. Take time off when necessary and be fresh and recharged for the next political fight.

The road ahead is long, fraught with inevitable failures and disappointments. But the end result—victory—is there for our taking. It will require hard work and sacrifice, but the math is in our favor. We win on the issues, we win on demographics, we win on basic common decency and morality. What we need to do is organize.

And as we look around at the new passion and energy from the Resistance movement, we have no doubt that we are all up to the challenge.

ACKNOWLEDGMENTS

Thanks to every one of you fighting in this Resistance. You give us hope, inspiration, and purpose. This is our country, and we're not going anywhere.

MARKOS: First and foremost, I would like to thank my family—Elisa, best of wives, and best of women, and Ari and Eli, because they are the reason I fight every day. This is *their* world. I refuse to let Trump and his asshole Republicans trash it. My mother for instilling the values I carry to this very day, and my father for always being with me, even if just in spirit. Matthew Lewis for his amazing editing chops, both with the printed word and talking through some of these ideas. Michael Huttner for bringing me into this project and offering direction. Irna Landrum, Kerry Eleveld, and Wagatwe Wanjuki for their invaluable feedback. Adam and Lyn Werbach for their amazing retreat space. My top lieutenants, Will Rockafellow and Susan Gardner, for their friendship and guidance, and for giving me space to write this book, picking up my slack at work. The rest of the *Daily Kos* team for building our amazing little corner of the Internet. The *Daily Kos* community, for being the most amazing, most engaged, and most active online community *anywhere*. I refuse to take for granted their critical role in growing and empowering our movement, and I work diligently every day to be worthy of their trust. I am the luckiest person in the world for having all of these amazing people in my life.

MICHAEL: To Debbie for putting up with me all these years. And for taking such good care of our children when I've been on the road—thank you. To our son, Lee—who composed his first song, "A B C D E F G, Donald Trump is my enemy"—and our beautiful daughter and aspiring gymnast, Evy. They inspire me to make the world a better place. To Markos for writing the lion's share of this book and for being a dear friend and advocate for over a decade. To my mom for teaching me persistence and to my dad for our chats at Chili's. To my brother David for his blunt constructive advice and to my sister Stephanie—my first fan. To my besties the J-Crew. To my team at Fenton who are dedicating their lives to improving the world. To Jared Polis for being a true leader. To Jeff Shesol for his counsel and to Kris Pauls of Disruption Books for taking on this sprint. To Alan Franklin and Carrie Steele for always helping me and to Jacquelyn Davis and Jordan Day for always housing me. To the ProgressNow network of advocates, who continue to fight for progressive change in their communities. I am truly fortunate and thankful to have a supportive family and so many great friends.

ABOUT THE AUTHORS

MARKOS MOULITSAS is the founder and publisher of *Daily Kos*. Born in Chicago, he actually lived his early years in El Salvador until that nation's civil war forced his family back to the United States. A US Army veteran, Markos served as an artillery fire direction specialist, stationed in both Oklahoma and Bamberg, Germany. After earning two degrees at Northern Illinois University, Markos earned his JD at Boston University. He and his wife moved to Berkeley, California, in 1999, and still live there today with their two children. Follow him on Twitter @markos.

MICHAEL HUTTNER is a corporate and political strategist, attorney, and entrepreneur. He recently served as the CEO of Fenton, the global social change agency. He previously served as president of the Huttner Group Inc., a Boulder-based firm that helps solve complex financial, communications, and public policy problems in a variety of industries. Michael has helped launch over forty different political organizations and has led communications "war rooms" for political and private clients. Michael also is the founder of ProgressNow, a network of state-based communications organizations that moves people to action through communications and digital media. Described as the "crown jewel" of progressive investors' efforts to build messaging power in the states, ProgressNow continues to expand, with more than 3.4 million members in twenty-three states. Previously, Michael worked as policy adviser to Governor Roy Romer and clerked at the Clinton White House for the Office of the Counsel to the President. He earned his JD from the University of California Hastings Law School and his BA from Brown University.

CPSIA information can be obtained
at www.ICGtesting.com
Printed in the USA
BVOW09s1107130817
491733BV00004B/15/P